D0235279

THE
FIGHTER PILOT'S
HANDBOOK

THE
FIGHTER PILOT'S HANDBOOK

MAGIC, DEATH AND GLORY IN THE
GOLDEN AGE OF FLIGHT

GORDON THORBURN

metro

First published by Metro Publishing,
an imprint of
John Blake Publishing Limited
3 Bramber Court, 2 Bramber Road
London W14 9PB

www.johnblakepublishing.co.uk

www.facebook.com/johnblakebooks ∎
twitter.com/jblakebooks ∎

First published in hardback in 2015

ISBN: 978-1-78418-819-1

British Library Cataloguing-in-Publication Data:

A catalogue record for this book is available from the British Library.

Design by www.envydesign.co.uk

Printed in Great Britain by CPI Group (UK) Ltd

1 3 5 7 9 10 8 6 4 2

Papers used by John Blake Publishing are natural, recyclable products made
from wood grown in sustainable forests. The manufacturing processes
conform to the environmental regulations of the country of origin.

Every attempt has been made to contact the relevant copyright-holders, but
some were unobtainable. We would be grateful if the appropriate people
could contact us.

CONTENTS

ACKNOWLEDGEMENTS

The jacket illustration, which is by Captain W E Johns, is from the artwork for the jacket of his first *Biggles* collection, *The Camels Are Coming*, first published in 1932. It, and the extract from *Biggles of 266* (1934) on page 2, are reproduced by permission of Rogers, Coleridge & White Ltd on behalf of the Estate of Captain W E Johns.

Grateful thanks also to John Lester, editor of *Biggles Flies Again* (http://www.bigglesfliesagain.com) and of the website of The W. E. Johns Appreciation Society (www. wejas.org.uk), and to Roger Harris (www.biggles.com), for their help with the jacket artwork for this book.

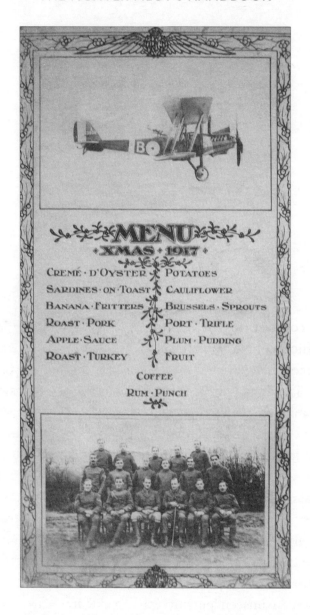

This is the menu for the officers' mess, No. 9 Squadron, Royal Flying Corps, Christmas 1917. The biplane is a Royal Aircraft Factory RE8, known as the 'Harry Tate'. Note the upward-firing exhaust pipe just in front of the pilot. What exactly 'Cremé d'Oyster' was has puzzled French scholars for almost a century.

PREFACE

In contrast to the treats lined up for those lucky officers of No. 9 (pictured opposite), it looked like being a turkey-free Christmas dinner in the officers' mess, No. 266 Squadron, until Second Lieutenant Bigglesworth remembered flying over a flock of turkeys somewhere behind enemy lines. He thought he'd go and liberate one.

He landed his Sopwith Camel in a field by the farm. After several alarums, during the description of which we learn that our intrepid hero weighed ten stone, which makes him smaller than we imagined, he took off, struggling in the tiny cockpit to contain the violent protests of a very large turkey, all alive-o, and pursued by small-arms fire from German soldiers.

Soon in unseen pursuit was an Albatros fighter (aka *Haifisch*, shark), probably a D Mark 5, called the V-strutter for its wing-strut arrangement, possibly one of the new Mark 5As, or possibly even an old Mark 3 (also a V-strutter).

The turkey by now had got itself wedged between pilot and seat-back, in which unfortunate position it absorbed a few bullets from the specially lightened LMG08/15 version of the Spandau 7.9mm machine gun that would otherwise have killed Biggles. Assessing the situation in an instant, Biggles stowed the dead and therefore manageable turkey on the cockpit floor and turned his undivided attention to his attacker.

> Biggles spun the Camel round in its own length and shot up in a climbing turn that brought him behind the straight-winged machine. That the pilot had completely lost him he saw at a glance, for he raised his head from his sights, and was looking up and down, as if bewildered by the Camel's miraculous disappearance.
> Confidently, Biggles roared down to point-blank range. The German looked round over his shoulder at the same moment, but he was too late, for Biggles' hand had already closed over his gun-lever.
> He fired only a short burst, but it was enough. The Albatros reared up on its tail, fell off on to a wing, and then spun earthwards, its engine roaring in full throttle. [*Biggles of 266*, by Captain W E Johns, originally published in *The Modern Boy* in December 1934.]

By Christmas 1917 the Albatros D3, previously the best fighter at the Front, had lost its primacy, outperformed by the Sopwith Camel, the Royal Aircraft Factory SE5A and

By Christmas 1917, the Albatros D3 (pictured) was obsolete, outperformed by the Camel, the SE5A and other Entente machines, and the Albatros D5 was not a great deal better. By the time new types came in, it was too late for the German air force.

other Entente machines; and the Albatros D5 was not a great enough improvement. By the time new types came in, it was too late for the German air force.

The Camel was so manoeuvrable it could be unstable

in the wrong hands and quite a few learner pilots were killed in this aircraft. It could turn remarkably quickly to the right, helped by engine torque, but tended to go nose down, which Biggles obviously knew how to overcome.

The real 266 Squadron, formed at the end of the Great War, was disbanded a year later like so many and re-formed in December 1939 to fly Spitfires in the Battle of Britain. The squadron was disbanded for good in 1964.

William Earl Johns flew in the First World War but not in Sopwith Camels. Called up in 1914 as a Norfolk reserve soldier, he was with the Yeomanry at Gallipoli and the Machine Gun Corps at Salonika. In 1917 he received his commission as second lieutenant and his transfer to the Royal Flying Corps as trainee pilot.

The new Royal Air Force, established 1 April 1918, had Johns as a flying instructor but he was just in time to see some action when posted to 55 Squadron in August 1918, flying DH4 bombers into Germany.

The squadron raided Mannheim on 16 September. After taking damage from anti-aircraft fire, Johns was set upon by Fokker D7 fighters, said to be of Jasta 4, the unit of Ernst Udet (q.v.) and shot down, although not by Udet himself, who was on sixty victories at the time.

Johns, wounded, survived the crash but his observer did not, so the pilot stood alone in the dock at Strasbourg to be found guilty of indiscriminate bombing of civilian targets, a crime that carried the death penalty. Why the sentence was not carried out is uncertain; Johns was in a POW camp when the war ended.

He stayed in the RAF until 1927 with one promotion, from pilot officer to flying officer, the equivalent of army lieutenant, and began writing over a hundred Biggles stories in 1932 – but he never was a captain.

The real story that brought Biggles to life was as remarkable as any of his adventures. Imagine a fellow inventing the musket and showing it to His Lordship. 'I say,' says the impressed noble. 'Jolly useful, what? Could knock down no end of pheasants with that.'

'Yes, my lord,' says the inventor. 'But I have a cunning plan. What about using it in battle?'

'In battle? Good heavens, no. By the time you've reloaded, you'll have been run through. No, no. Swords and horses, that's what we want in battle. Swords and horses.'

It wasn't quite as one-eyed as that with aeroplanes; but it wasn't far off.

The Sopwith Camel was so manoeuvrable it could be unstable in the wrong hands. Note the dihedral angle (the upward angle from horizontal) of the lower wings, unlike the 'straight-winged machine' Albatros, which had no dihedral. This helped stability about the roll axis, or in the 'spiral mode'; but it is unlikely the full aeronautical significance of the dihedral effect was understood by the Camel's designers.

PART ONE

Aeroplanes? In a War?

THOMAS MOY AND HIS AERIAL STEAMER

Towards conquering gravity by machine rather than gas bag, most of the practical work was done between 1891 and 1905. Before that, there were always people wanting to imitate birds, flapping wings in an effort to fly, and as long ago as 1799 came the first theoretical description of the kind of machine people would need, if they were ever to be able to fly usefully.

Sir George Cayley, 1773–1857, Yorkshire baronet, lord of the manor of Brompton-by-Sawdon in the North Riding near Scarborough, set out the basic principles at that time and in a more detailed paper published in 1809. He understood that we should have to replace flapping wings with fixed ones, and that flying surfaces would need to be curved to produce sufficient lift to overcome the drag, that is, the combined weight of the flying machine, plus its burden of aeronauts, plus its motive force, an engine. Steam engines, he said, would never do, but some new sort of engine would be required, so that forward motion could generate the aforementioned lift and the craft could journey purposefully from A to B.

Without a suitable engine, Sir George built several gliders that worked, one of which was supposedly piloted by his coachman in 1853 down Brompton Dale, but the quest continued for powered flight.

Sir George's opinion on steam power did not deter two other Englishmen, William Henson and John Stringfellow. They patented their airliner in 1842 – The Aerial Steam Carriage – and founded their airline, The Aerial Transit Company, 'to convey letters, goods and passengers from place to place through the air'. Through their appeals for investment in the company they hoped to raise the money to build the machine but, for some reason, investors did not rush forward. All that ever came of it was a short indoor flight of a scale model but, credit where it is due, the thing did fly, and it was steam-powered.

There was a lot of publicity engendered by Henson and Stringfellow, doubtless stirring interest in a young clerk in a London stationery firm, Thomas Moy (1823–1910). Like many other pioneers, Moy knew what the problem was. You only have to see a piece of paper blowing along the street to realise that a lightweight, flattish object can fly, but how do you control that and make that flight useful?

Moy started, again like many others, by watching birds. In the 1860s he made some model 'wings', attached them to a body, and towed the device like a little submarine under the still waters of a canal, to study how the currents flowed around the components. To his surprise, his experiment was ruined when his bird-boat surfaced; he had, without realising it, invented the hydrofoil.

He joined the newly formed Aeronautical Society of Great Britain (later the Royal Aeronautical Society), gave a paper on his conclusions regarding the seemingly effortless soaring flight of the albatross, and he designed a flying machine. Unlike Henson and Stringfellow, he built it.

Rather than wait for the engineers working on internal combustion to come up with a practical answer, Moy decided to ignore Sir George. The Aerial Steamer, with a lightweight engine developed by Richard Shill running on meths, made its debut at the Crystal Palace in July 1875 (only one year before the four-stroke petrol engine appeared). It had no pilot and was tethered, in the manner that aeromodellers call round-the-pole, and its wing, made of bamboo and linen, had a span of 14 feet. With its raised tailplane, today's readers might be reminded of the Starship *Enterprise*. Its inventor estimated that, to lift off, warp speed needed to be 35mph on its 2,000-yard circular track. Despite a really clever engine design, giving it over 500rpm, the Steamer only managed 12 mph, partly because its own motion caused the fumes from the three forward meths burners to blow out the other three.

Thomas Moy had built his machine out of his own limited funds and could not raise any more. He tried turning the Steamer into a kind of helicopter, which didn't work, but he did make a small aircraft, a model, that could take off under its own power provided by rubber bands. Such a take-off, without any kind of extra launching, was a significant feat for its time but, like steam, rubber would never do.

Was the Moy Aerial Steamer the last attempt to fly by steam? No, it wasn't – see page 24.

OTTO LILIENTHAL AND HIS HANG GLIDER

The next idea to give a real boost to flying-machine development came from Germany around 1891, curiously enough by a return to the birdman strategy. Otto Lilienthal and his brother Gustav made a pair of wings to fit on a man's arms, as so many had before, but with a major difference. Otto, agreeing with Sir George on curvature but not on fixedness, had realised that the wings had to be convex above, concave beneath. He made hundreds of flights in birdman mode and began to develop more sophisticated machines.

By 1895, he was sitting in an aircraft that would be easily recognisable to hang-glider pilots today. It had a tail with plane and fin (see patent diagram), and it would fly when launched from the top of a hill carrying a chap in a Tyrolean hat.

Here comes Otto, the birdman of Brandenburg, leaping into the unknown.

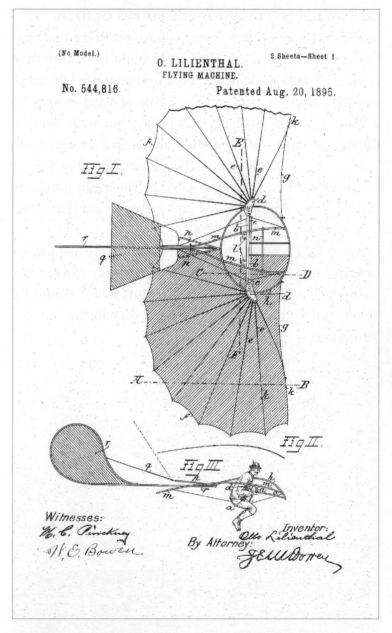

Having a feather in one's cap was definitely the thing for nineteenth-century hang-gliders.

Lilienthal published several papers, usually to little effect. Some official attitudes could be summed up as 'Man will never fly', while others stated that man would only fly if he could work out how to do it with flat wings. Lilienthal sent his ideas to Hureau de Villeneuve, president of a French scientific commission investigating the possibilities of aeronautics, who wrote back from Paris:

> I consider wings, pre-eminently, as moving organs for propelling at great speed, and when this speed has been reached the force necessary for supporting may be neglected. I have shown this by constructing mechanical birds with flat wings which fly very fast and keep themselves up very well when flying in the air. I try to make the wings true planes as far as I can, for the flatter they are the greater is the speed attained.

Lilienthal refused to join the flat-wing society and continued to publish his own ideas. In 1893 he wrote: 'Even to the present hour the majority of aviators expend much painful effort in attempting the hopeless task of trying to fly with flat wings.'

From the same paper, published in *Zeitschrift für Luftschiffahrt* (*Journal of Aviation*, literally 'airship travel' but meaning all types of aerial vessel) by *Deutsche Verein zur Förderung der Luftschiffahrt* (German Society for the Advancement of Aviation):

> I have now reached the close of a series of

experiments during which I had set myself a definite task. This was to construct an apparatus with curved carrying surfaces which should enable me to sail through the air, starting from high points and gliding as far as possible, that is to say, at the least obtainable inclination; and to do this with stability and safety even in winds of medium strength.

He succeeded in gliding but knew full well that this was only the beginning.

The mere discovery that with arched wings supporting forces are evolved which permit soaring to be performed with little effort is far from being the final invention of flying. The successful practical utilisation of this important phenomenon in air resistance is going to demand a considerable amount of ingenuity. To get the upper hand over the wind with flying machines and to bring about a beneficial utilisation of those favourable supporting forces, for such a task many a technical man will have a chance to throw his talent into the scale; for the field of work lying before us is no small one.

As to his own talents, Lilienthal continued to believe they were best directed towards the imitation of bird flight. He intended to develop it gradually, from flexing wing tips inwards to fully beating wings, but saw there might be other ways.

The only method which, in my opinion, might to a certain degree offer the advantages of moving wings is that of rotating air propellers, which lift and propel at the same time. I have already expressed my opinion in the past that possibly good results may be obtained with such devices if skilfully worked out. Actual trial alone can decide this question, as we must let the air and the wind have their say in the matter. For this reason it would be desirable to have some such ideas carried out in practice, so that there will be an end to fruitless discussions.

None of Lilienthal's flights was very long but he made a great many, over 2,000 by the time of his death in 1896 from injuries sustained when his latest machine collapsed in mid-air. Photographs of him, doing what nobody had done before with such success, had been in newspapers and magazines around the world. Many technical men were inspired to throw their talents into the scale.

CLÉMENT ADER AND HIS STEAM BOMBER

The Frenchman Clément Ader, a contemporary of Lilienthal, was also a curved wing proponent. He tried the birdman approach to flight as a youth, in a kind of winged kite he had made. He frightened himself out of trying again but never lost his fascination with the notion of flying.

While studying the techniques of storks and vultures, he set about making himself wealthy enough to devote time and money to flying machines, and he did that in the new industries, as a telephone pioneer and inventor of rubber tyres for velocipedes. He also developed an early form of the caterpillar track – but his passion was up above.

In 1886 he set about his first aircraft. It took him four years to build. On 9 October 1890, he powered up the steam engine, got in the craft and, according to witnesses, made a short hop, perhaps as much as sixteen feet, perhaps as high as eight inches.

The Ader Éole (named for Aeolus, Greek god of the winds) looked like a cross between a giant bat and a pleasure boat; its single propeller had blades like solid feathers. It probably did struggle through a touch-and-go power-glide but certainly not the 50-metre flight that Ader claimed, before crashing in a heap. It was not a controlled, sustained flight or landing.

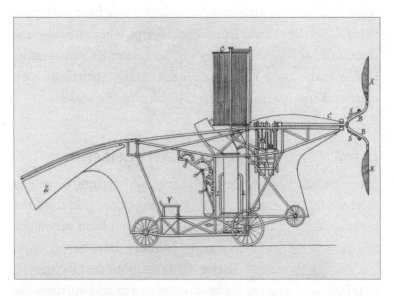

The Ader Éole is shown in a contemporary illustration, flying, with a gentleman seated comfortably within. Like all of Ader's machines, it never really got off the ground and never landed either. All his 'flights' ended in crashes.

So far, the objective everywhere had been simply to fly, and nothing more. Ideas of what might be done in a flying machine could not be realised until the machine actually flew, and here Monsieur Ader thought himself well ahead of the game. By claiming rather more for his Éole than he should have, he convinced the forward-thinking French authorities to assign to him the task of designing a powered aeroplane with a potential for military use, as a bomber. The prime minister of the time, de Freycinet, declared the Éole to be 'an aerial scout and torpedo boat' and he and top army man General Mensier agreed with Ader that 'He shall be master of the world who is master of the air'.

A government contract was signed in 1892, by which Ader would receive payments amounting to three million francs if, as he said he would, he built an aircraft that could carry two men, flying several hundred metres above the ground, for at least six hours. Presumably this was the time estimated for Ader's bomber to get to Germany and back.

The eventual result, the Ader Avion 3, again steam powered, much more like a giant bat, less like a boat, with two propellers and many advanced technical features, was still far too heavy and much too susceptible to ill winds. On 12 October 1897, in front of Generals Mensier and Grillon and in unsuitable, gusty weather, it failed the test utterly.

Ever the optimist, Ader claimed an uninterrupted flight of 300 metres. The generals noted only that the back wheels left the ground a number of times before the machine veered off course and crashed in pieces. As Sir

George Cayley had pointed out a century before, steam engines would never do.

This was long before any other government was prepared to put money down on a heavier-than-air military project and the French concluded that they had jumped in too quickly. They withdrew all funding. Ader was heartbroken but built a copy of the Avion 3 that can still be seen at the Musée des Arts et Métiers in Paris.

HORATIO PHILLIPS AND HIS VENETIAN BLIND

In 1893, the British magazine *Engineering* published a detailed account of heavier-than-air flight achieved by a machine driven by Welsh coal. This aircraft, designed and made by Horatio Frederick Phillips, of Harrow, had curved wings too, but they were only an inch and a half wide. Admittedly, they were 22 feet long and there were fifty of them; they stacked one above the other in a stout wooden frame giving a combined aerofoil area of 136 square feet.

If Clément Ader saw the magazine he may have noted the excellent 'flying' speed achieved, of 28mph, but it was done as per Moy's method with a pilotless craft round-the-pole. The frame containing the fifty wings, or 'sustainers' as Horatio called them, was mounted crossways over a long, thin canoe in which sat the engine, and forward motion was supplied by a propeller like a double-bladed oar. The canoe was fixed at its prow to a circular wooden track, but 'flew' when the stern left the ground.

'That the machine can not only sustain itself, but an added weight, was demonstrated beyond all doubt, even under the disadvantages of proceeding in a circle, with the wind blowing pretty stiffly,' said *Engineering*, but the machine had no means of steering in any direction, no means of take-off or landing, and was not big enough to carry a man.

Encouraged, Phillips built more flying machines and moved on from steam to internal combustion engines. His first attempt at manned flight was his 1904 twenty-winger, which had a tail for stability and managed a 50-foot hop. His 1907 machine had two hundred wings on four frames and looked like it would make a good shed on wheels if the walls and roof were finished. Amazingly, Horatio flew 500 feet in this, without any kind of control, before crashing; but he realised that his basic principle would never be the way forward, and he gave up.

The Phillips 1907 Multiplane: curved wings might indeed be the future, but not as a powered Venetian blind.

OCTAVE CHANUTE, AUGUSTUS HERRING AND THEIR COMPRESSED AIR PLANE

As well as motive power, another great problem to be solved was stability and control in the air. Lilienthal had exerted control by shifting his body weight, as modern hang-gliders do, and recommended that novices flying his type of machine should acquire this skill as second nature before trying anything adventurous.

A Frenchman and naturalised American was commissioned to help design a multi-wing birdman machine which could be controlled, to an extent, by moving the flying surfaces rather than the pilot. He was Octave Chanute, a civil engineer and aeronautical evangelist, who would surely have known about Cayley and certainly knew about Lilienthal, as he published the German's work in New York in 1894. After having several Lilienthal-type soarers made and tested, Chanute went on with his collaborator and chief designer, Augustus Moore Herring, to produce the Chanute-Herring glider in 1896, recognisably a fixed wing biplane with curved aerofoils, foreshadowing most of what was to come for the next thirty years.

Experiments with a compressed-air engine were only partially successful, as explained by an account of Herring's first motorised flight in November 1898, at St Joseph, Michigan, in the *Chicago Record*. Professor Herring of New York was described as a scientist of national reputation and an extensive writer on aeronautical subjects. The reporter went into the shed to have a look.

> [His] flying machine hung suspended by four wires from the ceiling. It consisted of two

21

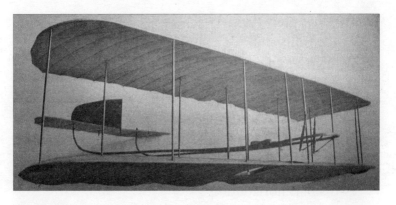

Recognisably a curved-aerofoil biplane, Herring was so taken with the glider that he believed that all there was to do now was fit an engine of some sort, and a propeller.

long surfaces or aerocurves, which resemble broad, shallow gutters turned upside down and spaced one above the other about a yard apart. These surfaces in themselves are marvels of construction. They are of the thinnest china silk, stretched over very light curved wooden ribs, and varnished with a transparent shrinking varnish, which stretches the silk without a single wrinkle, to the tightness of a drumhead. These surfaces are then trussed together, one above and one below by a number of upright posts. Then diagonal steel wires make the machine resemble a miniature bridge which by its extreme rigidity and lightness shows the highest skill of the mechanical engineer.

Just above the lower surface of this is a small two-cylinder engine, weighing perhaps a dozen pounds, but which, if necessary, can develop four or five horsepower. This engine turns two five-foot propellers, set parallel and situated one at the front and one at the rear of the machine. Below the engine is a small tank six or seven inches in diameter and about two feet long. This is filled with compressed air at a pressure of 500 pounds to the square inch, furnishing power to the engines. Even with the tank, about twenty inches below the bottom surface, are two small horizontal bars which in flight carry the operator's weight. Further out on each side and extending still farther down are four small upright posts which support the machine on skids. At the back of the whole machine are two surfaces intersecting at right angles and which are joined to the main apparatus to act as an automatic regulative mechanism.

When the craft was taken out of one of the world's first aircraft hangars,

Mr Herring crawled underneath the apparatus and raised it so easily that it seemed to possess no weight at all. A few forward steps were made, the engine shrieked and the machine leaped forward, an instant later sailing in free air, with the skids nearly a yard above the sand and the operator's legs drawn up in a bunch near the tank.

It was really flying, already the machine covered a distance of fifty or sixty feet when the speed perceptibly slacked and a little farther on the apparatus came gently to rest on the sand. The distance covered was afterward measured at seventy-three feet and the time of flight was estimated by Herring at eight to ten seconds. He explained, however, that though this represents a speed of only five or six miles an hour over ground, the real speed of the machine was more nearly thirty miles an hour, as it was advancing against a twenty-five mile wind.

Anyone who ever built a Keil Kraft scale model aeroplane, powered by a rubber band, will understand what was going on that day in St Joseph. Anyone who ever played cricket will wonder at something that took ten seconds to travel very little more than the length of the pitch.

Mr Herring expresses himself as well pleased with the results so far obtained and he expects to continue experiments with a machine capable of much longer flight next season. He feels that this experiment leaves little question of the possibility of building a machine which will fly and carry its operator. He considers it unlikely, however, that flying machines will ever carry freight or more than one or two persons at a time.

MAGNIFICENT MEN AND THEIR NON-FLYING MACHINES

In 1901, Frank Hornby patented his Improved Toy or Educational Device for Children and Young People,

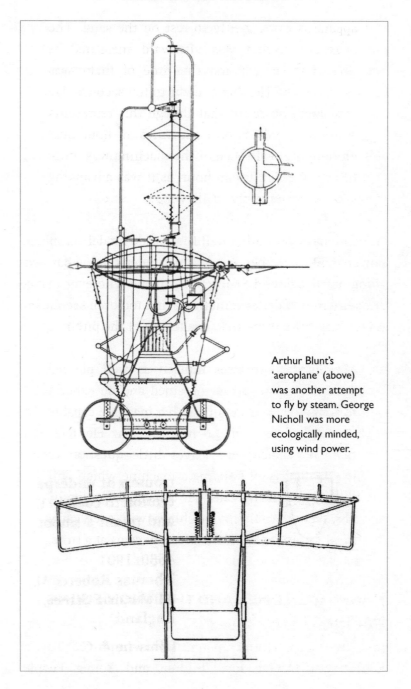

Arthur Blunt's 'aeroplane' (above) was another attempt to fly by steam. George Nicholl was more ecologically minded, using wind power.

by which 'children can construct mechanical objects, buildings etc. from independent pieces'. In the same year, John Turnbull patented his Self-Emptying Spittoon for the Floors of Railway Carriages, Thomas Roberts his Improved Means for Holding the Backs of Shirts in Position, and Allen Kerr his Improved Means of Exhibiting Advertisements, which 'causes the movement imparted to a toilet roll as a leaf is withdrawn for use to actuate means of bringing a fresh advertisement into view'.

While Frank Hornby's Meccano lives for ever, those other inventions, intriguing as they might be, went the same way as Arthur Henry Philip Blunt's Improved Flying Machine.

Arthur was a civil engineer and surveyor, living at 98 Albert Street, Regents Park, London NW, near Mornington Crescent underground station. Today, there is no plaque on the wall celebrating his Improved Machine, perhaps because it never flew and may not even have been built.

'It is driven by steam, propelled by the downward stroke of the propellers tilting the rear of the aeroplane upwards; gravity causes the machine to move in an inclined plane downwards and gather way enough to carry it upwards when the rear of the aeroplane is depressed. The propellers may also serve to force the machine forwards by inclining them downwards towards the front.'

Depressing the rear is only another way to describe pulling up the nose, which is what all modern aircraft do.

'The steering is partly effected by the aeronaut putting his weight on one or other of the cords from which the car hangs.'

It's a pity we don't have a view from the front, so we

could see the wings of the 'aeroplane', possibly represented here in cross-section by the oval shape in the middle of the diagram on page 25. It looks as if Arthur has foreseen the Wright Brothers' out-front elevator, but there's not much else to indicate successful flight.

George Nicholl's Improved Machine, on the other hand, does appear as if it might have done something or other, if only it hadn't been a cross between a bird and a perpetual motion device.

George was a mathematical instrument maker, living at 153 High Holborn, London WC, and his idea consisted 'essentially in providing one or more articulated members so constructed and arranged that they can be caused to vibrate by the action of the wind and thereby supply or assist in supplying the necessary motive power for propelling the machine. The machine is constructed of a framework with a roof of bamboo, metal etc., with a propeller at the rear.'

Covering himself in case the perpetual motion notion didn't exactly do the necessary: 'The propeller is operated by wind and a spring after the machine has attained a certain momentum, or by hand or by a motor'.

Another optimist, George even looked forward to the requirements of returning to earth, once aloft. 'Spring loaded legs deaden the shock on landing.'

And, if that didn't work, 'When not required to carry a person, the machine may be held captive in the manner of a kite'.

Baden Fletcher Smyth Baden-Powell, younger brother of the famous Scoutmaster, patented an Improved Aërial Machine in 1903, modestly terming himself a major in the Scots Guards when he was at the time President of the Aeronautical Society. Showing the same kind of spirit his brother brought to scouting, his machine would have rivalled the Big Dipper in buttock-clenching thrills, as it was 'a car or boat' fitted with wings and wheels, that hurtled down a steep railway track and (he expected) flew off at the end like a ski jumper.

Once in the air, 'the movements of the machine may be to some extent steered and controlled', and 'a sheet of water may be used to break the fall in case of accident'.

You have to admire the man's confidence. His device, which to some extent could be controlled, 'may be used either for studying aërial navigation or for recreational purposes'. Navigating in aircraft would be a major problem for another forty years at least, so we can express regret that the art was not studied more in those pioneering times by Baden-Powell.

The brothers Haylock, David and Richard, also in 1903, believed they had solved the problem of flight with their Self-Lifting Machine, which used vertically mounted, cylindrical Archimedean screws to take the aeronaut up, and horizontal ones to take him forward. 'These lifting fans, when not revolving, act as parachutes.'

How they might be made to revolve was not specified, but it would be with Malcolm Campbell Macleod's New Method of Giving Impetus to Flying Machines and the Like. This was in 1905, so heavier-than-air flight had been achieved and Mr Macleod, Gentleman, of South Kensington merely wanted to speed it up a bit. Anticipating Hitler's V1 doodlebug, his patent specified the use of cylinders filled with explosives. The result of 'the chemicals being fired by electricity or other means' would be 'an enormous impetus in an upward and forward direction'.

Whether the wire, fabric and wood aircraft of the day would have withstood 'an enormous impetus' is a matter for conjecture.

Possibly the most magnificent of all the non-flying machines, improved or otherwise, was the one proposed by Joseph de Lipkowski, engineer, of 104 Boulevard de Courcelles, Paris. This 'aërial machine', he said, 'consists essentially in two contra-rotating helical lifting planes which take the machine *up*, and a propeller which pulls it *forward*.'

Like George Nicholl before him, he foresaw the necessity of catering to passenger comfort. 'Pneumatic buffers deaden the shock on landing.' We can say that if Joseph's machine ever did need to land, we should want more than buffers to deaden the shock.

'The resistance which the rudder offers to the wind compensates for the action of the wind upon the lifting screws so that perfect equilibrium may be obtained.' So stable would the machine be in flight that it would stay upright in all weathers and at all speeds, or, as Joseph put it, 'the main axis of the apparatus may be so rendered vertical whatever be the velocity of its translation'.

Ah well, never mind, Arthur, George, Joseph and the rest. Wilbur and Orville were on the case.

AMERICA AND HER AIR FORCE

It would be the Wright Brothers, Wilbur and Orville, who would make that final leap. They were in long and detailed

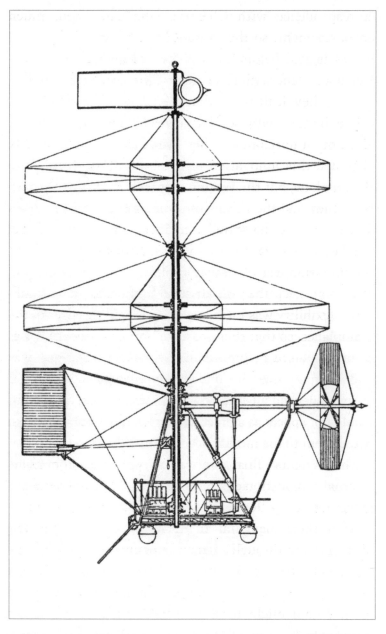

In Joseph de Lipkowski's design, no particular motive power is designated although internal combustion looks the most likely.

correspondence with Chanute, who gave them much encouragement, so they would have been fully aware of what had gone before. They virtually copied the Chanute-Herring biplane with three major differences.

First, they dealt with what the *Chicago News* reporter called the automatic regulative mechanisms, by adding an elevator, or horizontal rudder. Most later designs swiftly switched this innovation to the back of the craft, onto the tailplane, but the Wrights put it in front of the wings. Now they had the means of steering the machine up or down. Chanute had tried something similar by rocking whole wings on a horizontal axis. It hadn't worked but the intention was obviously good.

To help keep the aircraft level and enable it to bank-turn, flexibility was introduced to the trailing edges of the mainplanes, so that those parts of port or starboard wings could be raised or dipped in flight. The technique was wing-warping, twisting one trailing edge up and the other down; independent ailerons had been thought about but would not appear as a practical device until Henri Farman fitted them to his modified Voisin in 1908.

The Wrights' final innovation was a custom-made internal combustion engine developing 12 horsepower and powering a propeller behind, to push the aircraft along.

After their inaugural flight in December 1903, the brothers went through a largely experimental 1904 but, by the end of 1905, they had made almost 50 flights, including one in Flyer 3 covering 24½ miles in something over half an hour. Wilbur might have gone further if he had not run out of petrol.

Now the race was on. Little was known to science about

the forces that affect a flying machine, about airflow, about the relationship between performance and the size and shape of wings, tail, fuselage, propeller, or about the true influence of those regulative mechanisms, automatic or manual. Everything was experimental, trial and error, and very, very exciting.

Records were broken almost as soon as they were made. Before 1905, nobody had been able to fly for half an hour. By 1908, everybody was doing it. The French pioneers Blériot and the Farmans were making flights of twenty miles and more. The Farman brothers, Maurice, Henri and Richard, were (like most aero pioneers) of a dare-devilish inclination. Maurice and Henri started by winning cycle races and went on to motor cars and Grands Prix before graduating to the ultimate in thrills and spills, flying.

Wilbur Wright was in France too and, in front of senior military gentlemen, took the ex-Governor of French Indo-China for a flight of ten minutes. He went to Germany where he taught many eager pupils how to fly. According to the *New York Times*, he left those pupils eminently able to teach others to operate a Wright machine.

After recording the first flight with a female passenger in October 1908, in the November he set an altitude record of 82 metres, and a month later took the French AeroClub 100 metre altitude challenge and beat it by ten metres. As well as height he made distance and duration records, winning the first Coupe de Michelin and $5,000 for the longest flight of the year, minimum qualifying distance 12 miles. Wilbur set a world record of 90 miles.

Wilbur foresaw military employment for his machines. He said: 'As a military aid, the aeroplane has proved itself most successful and this is the greatest feature of the flying machine today', but the American authorities were not so keen. Without the aggressive impetus of impending war, progress was slow and steady.

The US Army formed an Aeronautical Unit in 1907, part of the Signals Corps, when signals officers tended to think mostly about tethered balloons. Even so, in the November of that year, the War Department assigned the mighty sum of $25,000 to buy an aeroplane.

The spec was tight: the machine must carry two men for 125 miles without stopping, at 40mph. It must be capable of flying in any direction under control of the pilot, and of landing without damaging itself or its crew.

The Wright brothers were the obvious favourites for the contract but, up in Canada, under the sage guidance of Alexander Graham Bell, the Aerial Experiment Association had recently been formed. It was an interesting coming-together of minds and abilities. Mrs Mabel Bell, Alexander's wife, provided the money; two young engineers, Casey Baldwin and John McCurdy, provided the fearlessness and the DIY skills, and Glenn Curtiss the knowledge of motors. A further recruit, through the good offices of President Theodore Roosevelt, was a government representative, Signals Corps Lieutenant Thomas Etholen Selfridge. He had piloted an airship and was interested in aeroplanes, so that made him the army expert

One of the first things the Association did was fly a kite. Before Wilbur and Orville, the main and universal problem with flying machines was that if they were big enough to carry a man, they were too heavy to fly very far, or at all. Ignoring what was happening elsewhere, it was Bell's pet idea that he could overcome this difficulty with a tetrahedral kite made out of thousands of little tetrahedron cells. Do you know the Toblerone chocolate bar? Imagine a giant one of those. Or, imagine a house roof with triangular gable ends. Take the roof off the house, tilt it so that the open underside is into the wind, and pull it along.

The lucky pilot on 6 December 1907 was the lieutenant. They towed the kite, named Cygnet 1, over a lake with a motor boat. It stayed up for seven minutes.

Whether the CO of the Signals Corps knew about this we cannot tell, but a couple of weeks later he sent out the official request for a heavier-than-air flying machine, for which he already had the $25,000.

The Wright brothers remained top of the list when the Aerial Experiment Association's first aeroplane, Red Wing, built by Baldwin to designs by Selfridge and piloted by Baldwin, crashed after twenty seconds in March 1908.

That May, Red Wing's successor, White Wing, was launched with high hopes. It had hinged ailerons controlled, as with Otto's hang-gliders, by straps attached to the pilot. When he leaned this way, the aircraft went this way. It had wheels rather than skids, a Curtiss engine, and it flew for more than 300 yards with Baldwin in it. Selfridge had already flown it for 100 feet, making him the first American military pilot. Next time, McCurdy took it up and wrecked it.

Four months later, the Wrights were flying for an hour and more, and Selfridge went with Orville as passenger in the latest machine, called the Model A, the familiar

Wright-style pusher biplane with elevators out front but with a more powerful engine at 28hp. Although more than thirty of the Model A were built, in the USA, UK and (mainly) Germany, this proved to be as far as development could go of the first really successful aircraft design. The Model B and subsequent letters, the Burgess-Wright variants made in co-operation with yacht and aircraft builder Starling Burgess, were basically the same and high speeds could never be achieved with huge elevators sticking out before.

After a successful few circuits, Model A1's propeller fractured and it crashed, at Fort Myer, Virginia, on 17 September 1908, while Wilbur was in France. Orville was badly hurt and Selfridge died of head injuries, becoming the world's first aeroplane fatality. He might have survived had he been wearing some sort of helmet.

This is Lieutenant Selfridge in a Wright Flyer. He would become the first person to be killed in an aeroplane crash.

Another Model A, strengthened and thoroughly tested, became the US Army's Airplane Number One in July 1909, and by January 1910 army officers were dropping little bags of sand from it to simulate bombing. Later in that year, an officer called Fickel fired a rifle from it, although we don't know at what, and Theodore Roosevelt went up in it. He had become an ex-President in 1909 but a President of the USA is for ever Mr President, so he became the first President to fly in an aircraft.

Glenn Curtiss had been busy the while and he concentrated on the navy. While Mr Roosevelt was earning his wings, a civilian called Eugene Ely was taking off in a 50hp Curtiss aircraft from a platform built over the bow of the light cruiser USS *Birmingham*. He landed on terra firma but the idea of aircraft carriers was established and Curtiss, casting bread upon the waters, offered free pilot training for one navy officer. Lieutenant T Gordon 'Spuds' Ellyson thus became US Naval Aviator One.

More firsts came now in rapid succession. Ely landed a Curtiss on a ship. Curtiss built float planes. The first photo-reconnaissance was a flop because the guinea-pig troops hid in the woods. Lieutenant Parmelee piloted the Wright Flyer while observer Lieutenant Crissy dropped a grenade at a practice target in January 1911, which was the first dropping of live explosive from an aeroplane, but we don't know if he hit.

Robert Collier, owner of *Collier's Magazine*, possibly the first person to buy a private aeroplane, loaned his Wright Flyer to the army by way of encouragement to them to embrace aviation as a military tool. Lieutenants Foulois and Parmalee flew it for 106 miles nonstop, dropping messages as if to forces on the ground.

In November 1912, a demonstration showed how an aircraft could 'spot' for artillery by signalling with Very lights, and in March 1913 the first US military aviation unit was formed, Headquarters 1st Aero Squadron (Provisional), in a field near Texas City.

There had been many crashes and several deaths and bad injuries in pusher aircraft, so an army committee said there should be no more pushers, but it was only a recommendation.

As the war began in Europe, the United States, with no intention whatever of being involved, was quite happy to reorganise the US Army 1st Aero Squadron at San Diego, with eight aeroplanes and about a hundred men, of which sixteen were officers.

LOUIS BLÉRIOT AND HIS 33 MINUTES

In July 1909, Louis Blériot, with two years' experience of teaching himself to fly aircraft that he had taught himself to design and modify, plus some years of experiments before that (mostly failures), won £1,000 by flying a monoplane between Calais and Dover in poor weather. Here is the *Manchester Guardian* report of 26 July:

> It was done, moreover, in the short period of 33 minutes, the start being made at 4.35 a.m. and the descent at 5.08 a.m. The distance traversed was 26 miles or more, the bee-line distance being 22 miles.

It was nearly half-past four yesterday morning when the news reached Dover that M. Blériot contemplated making the flight, and a few minutes later came a wireless message stating that he was actually on his way across the French coast, having ascended at Baraques, a village two miles to the west of Calais. The monoplane travelled with great rapidity, and its motor made such a din that it was heard when it must have been six or seven miles from Dover.

M. Blériot's great bird-like machine was first sighted over the Channel to the eastward of Dover, heading for St. Margaret's Bay... it suddenly came round with a fine sweep to the westward, still at a high rate of speed. Strange as it may seem, the monoplane, now that it was heading westward, was travelling against a fresh south-west twenty-mile-an-hour breeze, but this appeared to cause no diminution in the rate of travel.

When about a mile out at sea the monoplane was judged to be flying at a height of about 300 feet... making a course for the opening in the cliffs behind the castle. On the cliffs M. Fontaine, a friend of Blériot's, had taken up position with a large French tricolour which he waved vigorously as the monoplane came over the harbour. M. Blériot was looking for this to guide him to the place where he wanted to come down. He steered the monoplane for the opening in the cliffs with as much ease as if it were a motor-car.

That Blériot did not follow the bee-line of 22 miles was due to a problem aircrew would suffer for years. In poor visibility, following a line decided near Calais when he saw a French destroyer sailing for Dover, with no other methods of guidance, he was blown off track by the wind to the east and his first sight of land was the beach at Deal. Still, he had said he would go to Dover so he flew the extra miles. In landing, he was buffeted by eddies and had to belly-flop from 65 feet, crumpling his craft a little, but never mind that.

Despite having promised his wife that he wouldn't do it, he'd done it, and much to the disappointment of the favourite for the race, another Frenchman, Hubert Latham. Latham had already tried but failed while becoming the first person to crash a serviceable aeroplane (the *Antoinette 4*) on water. Latham was actually waiting for a break in the weather – just two miles away from Blériot – for another attempt, in his *Antoinette 7*, when Blériot went for it. Apparently Latham's crew slept through the early-hours opportunity.

That prize, taking an average between prices and earnings, would be worth about £250,000 today, and the winning of it raised some disturbing questions for the *Daily Mail*, the newspaper that had offered it, and anyone else who gave the matter a little thought. If a Frenchman could fly to England but, as yet, no Englishman could fly to France, did not that make Great Britain vulnerable to attack from the skies?

Of course, the country was already vulnerable to attack by airship, and that type of aircraft seemed to be most favoured. They could fly ten times as far as M. Blériot

Blériot's Channel-crosser. In case he had to ditch, the propeller blades had obviously been designed to double as oars.

Four years later, Royal Flying Corps pilots were going to war in this, the Mark II, a much more sophisticated version.

and much higher. For a while, therefore, heavier-than-air machines remained a novelty numbering a few hundred in the world. Biggles was still at school. Even in his dreams he could not have imagined himself roaring around the sky shooting up other aircraft. Such a thing was no more possible than sitting in an armchair at home watching electric moving colour pictures of a talent contest.

GIULIO GAVOTTI AND HIS CELESTIAL ASSAULT

Eight years after the Wright Brothers flew a machine heavier than air, Italian ambitions in north Africa led to the first ever military use of such machines. Italy had that capability because, unlike most senior officers in other armies, theirs were enthusiastic about the possibilities of flight. In mid-1910, after a distinguished British general had told the Imperial Defence Committee that reconnaissance from the air would be futile, the Italian ministry of defence put together a budget of 10 million lire for a specialist unit of eight aircraft. This decision also ignored the worthies of the British Admiralty, who had said that aeroplanes were never likely to be useful to the Royal Navy but if they did prove so, the number needed would be no more than two.

Diplomatic tensions and internal pressures were building over the coastal regions of Libya, then known as Tripolitania and Cyrenaica, including the cities of Tripoli and Benghazi. These areas had long been occupied by the Ottoman Turks but were considered by the Italians to be under their sphere of influence and an opportunity for colonial expansion unavailable elsewhere. There was a well-established Italian trading population in Tripoli, which gave their home government the excuse it needed.

Turkey would not give way, so Italy declared war on 29 September 1911. On that day, the Italian air force consisted of two Blériot II, three Nieuport 4G, two Etrich Taube, two Farman, eleven pilots and thirty support staff.

The Nieuport was a monoplane like the Blériot but looking much more stylish to our eyes. In fact, it was a more advanced design, as a Russian pilot would prove in 1913 by performing the first loop-the-loop in one. This was Lieutenant Pyetr Nikolayevich Nesterov, on 27 August over Kiev. In the September, one of Blériot's test pilots, Adolphe Pégoud, destined to become the first fighter ace in the world, flew upside down and performed loops and rolls that had not been thought possible. Nesterov was arrested for endangering government property but released when Pégoud's loop was reported in the papers. The Frenchman was also the first pilot to make a parachute jump (in 1913) but it is not recorded if he had one with him when looping.

No looping could ever have been done in the Italians' two Etrich craft, Austrian-designed and made, called Taube (dove). The Taube monoplane had large wings with a wave-like profile, their upturned trailing edges looking like a pigeon's pinions. Herr Etrich is supposed to have based his design not on a bird but on the shapes of some exotic gliding seed pods of tropical trees, and this could certainly be the case. Manoeuvring was, however, more bird-like, achieved by a complex system of wing warping.

The Italians' Farmans were not, as we might have expected, the highly successful Maurice Farman 7 'Longhorn', produced in 1910 (and still in use in the war in 1915), but an earlier pusher-biplane design, probably the Farman 3, with the elevator mounted out front like the Longhorn and the original Wright machine. It had a biplane tail with no rudder fin, and relied for left/right steering on large flaps in the wings.

All of these aircraft had a service speed of around 50mph in level flight, in reasonable conditions; could reach maybe 60mph maximum and were single-seaters, although, at some point, a Blériot was modified as a two-seater.

The machines were loaded on board ship and taken to Libya as part of the invasion. The first military mission was flown on 23 October by the unit's commander, Captain Carlo Maria Piazza flying a Blériot, and the second the same day by Captain Riccardo Moizo flying a Nieuport. Both were on reconnaissance. Two days later, Captain

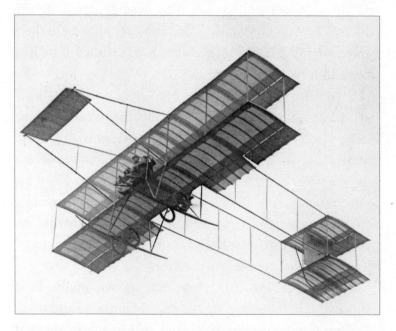

Hard as it is to believe, Italian pilots actually flew against the enemy in this machine, the Farman 3. Well, there wasn't very much else. The Farman Brothers' Model 3 set a world record in 1909 by flying 118 miles at an average speed of 36mph. A copy of this machine, the Bristol Box-kite, was the one flown by Bertram Dickson in 1910 (see below) and the first type purchased by the British army in 1911.

The Farman S7, aka Longhorn, was so-called for its front-mounted elevator after the fashion of the Wright Brothers. A 1910 design, the Longhorn was still in use in the war in 1915.

Moizo returned from another scouting trip with the wings of his aircraft pierced by three gunshots, so he had a first for that.

Come 1 November and Second Lieutenant Giulio Gavotti achieved another first. He had expected to fly reconnaissance missions, but here is an extract from his letter home:

> Today two boxes full of bombs arrived. We are expected to throw them from our planes. It is very strange that none of us have been told about this, and that we haven't received any instruction from our superiors. It will be very interesting to try them on the Turks.
>
> As soon as the weather is clear, I head to the camp to take my plane out [Etrich Taube]. Near the seat, I have fixed a little leather case

with padding inside. I have laid the bombs in it very carefully. These are small round bombs, weighing about a kilo-and-a-half each. I put three in the case and another one in the front pocket of my jacket.

Gavotti was heading for a camp at Ain Zara, east of Tripoli, then just an oasis, nowadays a town.

After a while, I notice the dark shape of the oasis. With one hand, I hold the steering wheel, with the other I take out one of the bombs and put it on my lap. I am ready. The oasis is about one kilometre away. I can see the Arab tents very well.

I take the bomb with my right hand, pull off the security tag and throw the bomb out, avoiding the wing. I can see it falling through the sky for couple of seconds and then it disappears. And after a little while, I can see a small dark cloud in the middle of the encampment. I have hit the target!

I then send two other bombs with less success. I still have one left which I decide to launch later on an oasis close to Tripoli. I come back really pleased with the result. I go straight to report to General Caneva. Everybody is satisfied.

Gavotti did something which had been banned by the Hague Convention of 1899, Declaration Number 1 referring to bombardment from balloons 'or by other new methods of a similar nature'. Only one or two of his grenades exploded, creating very little damage and no fatalities, but the headlines went around the wires of the world: 'Aviator Lt. Gavotti Throws Bomb on Enemy Camp. Terrorised Turks Scatter upon Unexpected Celestial Assault'.

This was many months after those two American aircrew, Lieutenants Parmelee and Crissy, dropped their practice grenade but this was different. This was a real target, and journalists prophesied the end of land and sea warfare, the dissolution of armies and navies, and a new era of celestial terrorism. H G Wells's 1908 science-fiction novel, *The War in the Air*, had come true. Then, they forgot all about it.

Later in that war, the Italian fliers scouted for navy and artillery, took photographs from the air, escorted their own troops while watching out for ambushes, and suffered the first fatality, Second Lieutenant Piero Manzini. He was shot down on a photographic mission; on such sorties, only one picture could be taken because the pilot could not change the camera plate and fly the aircraft at the same time. The second man into aeroplane war, Captain Moizo, became the first airman POW, after engine failure behind enemy lines.

Thus the Italian air force, with the first aeroplanes to go into battle, can claim to have been first at just about everything except for air combat, because the Ottoman Turks didn't have any aircraft, and bombing, because they dropped grenades, not self-detonating bombs. As to bombs, the Bulgarians were shortly to take the lead.

BERTRAM DICKSON AND HIS PROPHECY

On 16 October 1908 an American-born ex-showman, Samuel Franklin Cody (no relation to Buffalo Bill), attached to the British Army and working on kites and balloons, flew an aeroplane of his own design at Farnborough, for 1,390 feet (424m) in 27 seconds. This was the first officially recognised aeroplane flight in the United Kingdom and Cody confidently called his craft British Army Aeroplane No. 1. The flight ended in a crash. The army decided there was no future in such machines and there was no shortage of senior officers, army and navy, to predict that aeroplanes would never be any use in a war.

It was different over the Channel. Like the Italians, the French were advanced in their thinking concerning flying aeroplanes for military purposes. The French Army Air Service, *L'Aéronautique Militaire*, was formed in October 1910. Still, the majority didn't see the light: the Belgian army, for example, put together a Troop of Balloon Operators in 1909 (*Compagnie des Ouvriers et Aèrostiers*), bought an aeroplane in 1911- a Farman 3 -, but didn't designate an aeroplane section (*Compagnie des Aviateurs*) until 1913.

Watching the French with a suspicious eye, the German Army Air Service allowed a certain lowish priority to heavier-than-air craft, although what it really liked best was the Zeppelin *Luftschiff*.

Back in Britain, a considerable shift of opinion was brought about by Captain Bertram Dickson, a long-serving intelligence officer who caught the aeroplane bug in 1910. He learned to fly and decided to attach himself to the traditional annual manoeuvres occurring on Salisbury

Plain. Taking sides, he would act as aerial spy for Red Force, looking to locate Blue Force. When he did find them, he landed his Bristol Box-kite and notified Red Force HQ, apparently by telephone although where he found such a thing in 1910 is not clear, when public telephones were very rare outside the city and only one or two in a hundred homes were connected by private phone.

Anyway, when the resourceful captain came back to his aircraft, he was taken prisoner by a Blue Force corporal. Somehow he obtained his release, the umpires being unable to adjudicate on something with no precedent, and happened to run into Winston Churchill, recently made Home Secretary in the Asquith Liberal government. Dickson told Britain's youngest cabinet minister all about the importance of aeroplanes, militarily speaking.

Churchill had been demanding cuts in the defence budget so that more welfare reforms could be implemented, but his new job brought him into contact with the intelligence services. He became convinced of Germany's aggressive intentions, and he was already an aviation enthusiast (he would learn to fly in 1913), so the few flying visionaries in the armed forces now had a powerful ally.

In any case, Dickson's demonstration of air reconnaissance had made an impression. During 1911 an Air Battalion was formed by the Royal Engineers, including an Airship Company and an Aeroplane Company. Four Bristol Box-kites were purchased from the British and Colonial Aeroplane Company Limited. The Box-kite was a pusher, based on the French Voisin and the Farman 3, with a huge front-mounted elevator and a top speed of 40mph, and it looked more like a market stall on a windy day than an aeroplane, British or colonial. But it was a beginning.

In November 1911, with Lieutenant Gavotti's oasis attack already reported in the papers, Prime Minister Asquith commissioned his Technical Sub-Committee for Imperial Defence to report on the military potential of aeroplanes. This was the committee that, in the winter of 1908/9, had ordered the cessation of heavier-than-air experiments at military establishments. The Committee asked Bertram Dickson what he thought and, despite suffering from injuries sustained in the world's first mid-air collision (which would eventually kill him), he told them something quite remarkable:

> In case of a European war, between two countries, both sides would be equipped with large corps of aeroplanes, each trying to obtain information on the other. The efforts which each would exert in order to hinder or prevent the enemy from obtaining information would lead to the inevitable result of a war in the air, for the supremacy of the air, by armed aeroplanes against each other. This fight for the supremacy of the air in future wars will be of the greatest importance.

SIMEON PETROV AND HIS BOMB

The 1878 Treaty of Berlin recognised Romania, Serbia and Montenegro as states independent of the Ottoman Empire but didn't really sort out the boundaries of a newly defined and independent Bulgaria, which left considerable populations of Bulgarians in foreign lands -in Turkey, Romania and Serbia, and mostly in Macedonia. The situation could not last.

The Bulgarian government placed orders in early 1912 for some aircraft to go with their reconnaissance balloons, and sent a dozen army officers to France to be trained in flying, including Lieutenant Simeon Petrov. He gained local fame by gliding his machine in to land at the Blériot School after the engine had stopped, something nobody had done there before. Engine failures previously had led inevitably to crashes. He also developed an interest in aerial bombardment and began experimenting with modified grenades.

Any bomb Petrov might come up with would have to be dropped from the hand, so size was limited. Accuracy was a significant problem too, for aircrew who would want to stay as far away as possible from soldiers on the ground, small-arms fire being their most usual enemy peril. Petrov went back to archery for his answer, developing something like a very large, very fat dart, with a cruciate arrangement of a four-part flight behind an enlarged grenade body. If the true definition of 'bomb' supposes a detonator to set it off on impact, this wasn't one. It was a grenade, with a pin to pull out, so that was another factor to complicate the 'bomb'-aimer's life.

When the Bulgarians took delivery of their first aircraft in the summer of 1912, a Blériot naturally, the driver was Petrov, thus adding another innovation to his CV: the first person to fly over Bulgaria. More aircraft followed, acquired and flown home by those expat Bulgarian officers as political temperatures rose in the Balkans.

Serbia and Bulgaria had signed treaties and secret military agreements in the spring and early summer, partitioning Macedonia between them, and Bulgaria had been formally allied with Greece in May, the Greeks wanting territory back from the Ottomans in Thrace.

Now, at the end of September, they mobilised their armies. The Greeks flew reconnaissance missions over Thessaly on 5 October and German pilots working for the Ottomans flew similar ops over Thrace. The Balkan Alliance sent an ultimatum, in effect a declaration of war, to the Ottomans on 13 October, stating their demands regarding Macedonia. Almost immediately, they occupied undefended Turkish-held areas in what is now the Haskovo province of Bulgaria. Not far from Cisr-i Mustapha Pasha (Bridge of Mustapha Pasha, over the River Maritsa in modern Svilengrad), they established their airfield, which can be classified as the first to be so established on captured enemy territory.

According to a German account, in October 1912 Bulgaria had 23 aircraft, to wit: Blériot ten, Farman four, Albatros three, Nieuport two, Voisin, Sommer, Sikorsky and Bristol, one of each, all similar in performance to each other and all unreliable in the extreme. That Italians, Bulgarians or anyone else would be willing to go to war in one, must excite astonishment in every modern airman.

Most of the time, most of them were unserviceable, so numbers were important if any operations were to be flown. If accurate, a Bulgarian total of 23 represented a considerable feat of logistics and ingenuity on behalf of those returning pilots, since the army had only contracted for five Albatros machines ex-factory.

On Tuesday, 15 October 1912, orders arrived at the Mustapha Pasha airfield where, a murky, unpublishable photograph proves, at least nine aircraft were stationed. Next day, one was to be flown over the fortresses and artillery batteries surrounding the border town of Adrianople (modern Edirne), to ascertain Turkish strength. The defences were viewed as impregnable to conventional assault and the batteries included anti-balloon guns, which would surely be a grave danger to a frail aeroplane.

The mission was handed to pilot Radul Milkov and his observer Prodan Tarakchiev, who decided to take a couple of Petrov's bombs with them in their German-built Albatros F2, which was a modified copy of the Farman Longhorn.

Petrov had by this time tried several designs and had devised an impact detonator, but none of his bombs looked much like bombs as we might understand the word. One, a metre or more long, resembled a trophy for the pub darts team. Another might have been a model of a ship's propeller. Another resembled the orb in the Crown Jewels but three times the size, with giant arrow flights instead of the cross. We don't know which Milkov took.

Having reconnoitred the fort, they flew low over the railway station at Karagach and there Tarakchiev leaned over the side of his flimsy conveyance. At 50 or 60 miles an hour, aiming by eye only, he became the first man to drop a self-detonating bomb in anger. Damage was claimed.

With aircraft serviceability so poor, Petrov had plenty of time on the ground to think about bomb design, and chiefly he thought about accuracy. His final bomb, about a foot or 30cm long, was much more aerodynamic, with four smallish fins and a pointed nose on a cylindrical body. It weighed around six kilos and could blow a hole a metre deep and four or five metres across, which doesn't sound much but, to ground forces quite unused to this method of attack, it was terrifying. Regularly used during the siege of Adrianople, bombing caused far more havoc in the minds of the besieged than it did physical hurt, but its contribution to victory was considerable. It is probable that three aircraft were lost during the siege.

The Turkish commander eventually surrendered and matters were resolved elsewhere. Petrov sold his bomb design to the Germans.

NAVY BOYS AND THEIR FLYING SHIPS

When it was established on 13 April 1912, the Royal Flying Corps was to be in three parts. The Central Flying School trained pilots for the other two, the Military Wing and the Naval Wing, the word Military in this case meaning army. The new addition to His Majesty's armed services was not armed nor, according to many in the senior services, was it necessary.

It inherited a disorganised assortment of flying machines and balloons that had been gathered together in a fairly haphazard way by the Air Battalion of the Royal Engineers, and by the Admiralty, whose contribution included some aircraft donated from the private collection of a wealthy Irishman, Frank McClean. There was also an airfield-cum-flying school at Eastchurch in Kent, courtesy of Mr McClean.

McClean was famous for flying a 'hydro-aeroplane' under Tower Bridge and three more rather lower bridges, London Bridge, Blackfriars and Waterloo, just touching the water under the latter two. His machine was a Short seaplane, made by the company founded by the three brothers Oswald, Eustace and Horace Short, in which McClean had invested.

The Military Wing was initially structured in three squadrons, and No. 1 Squadron didn't have aeroplanes. They took over the balloons, airships and kites of No. 1 Airship Company of the Royal Engineers at Farnborough. No. 4 Squadron was formed in September, and by November the Wing had over fifty aeroplanes of many types, all fragile, all experimental, all frequently modified, and all liable to crash or suffer damage in some other way. Indeed, several fatal accidents in monoplanes led to a temporary ban on this configuration on 14 September 1912, but the majority were biplanes anyway.

No. 4 Squadron, for example, had five Bréguet types G3 and L2, some of which had been in service with the Royal Engineers, but this maker had no machines in the Naval Wing (three Bréguet seaplanes not delivered or not accepted) and neither was it popular with No. 4. The Bréguets were all called the coffee pot or the tin whistle for the unusual round and conical fuselage. They were partly controlled by wing-warping but you could also alter the angle of the wings with a spring-loaded device which, after being operated a number of times, could refuse to work at all, leaving the wings at a surprising angle of incidence, or it might become unsprung in a sudden gust rendering the machine temporarily out of control. Such events were not unique to this aircraft; all the wing-warpers could be temporarily disabled by wind-warping.

Between its foundation in 1912 and war in August 1914, the Naval Wing became the Royal Naval Air Service and the Military Wing assumed the full title of Royal Flying Corps, and they each acquired roughly 200 aircraft. The navy favoured mainly Short and Farman seaplanes but

A Bréguet held a record in 1911 for transporting eleven people five kilometres; quite how they all fitted into the coffee pot is not known, nor if they were university students. No. 4 Squadron's five were: one L1 (Renault 60hp engine), two L2 (pictured, Renault 70hp) and two G3 (Gnôme 100hp), but altogether only a few flying hours are recorded. The first one crashed, the second had three accidents needing repairs, the third crashed, the fourth hardly flew enough to have a crash, and the fifth crashed. None made it past 1913.

there were almost 40 different types in their 200; the army's chief equipment was the Royal Aircraft Factory BE2A but again, there were 30 other marques and models. This is not to say that either body ever had that many on strength, nor anywhere near that number simultaneously in serviceable condition, nor that any two aircraft supposedly the same were certain to be exactly alike.

In later times, one Spitfire Mark I was a precise copy of another. Nobody at the squadron aerodrome thought of altering the shape of the tail, or perhaps trying different wheels on the undercarriage or rearranging the cockpit, but that happened all the time with these early machines. To take one typical example: Short S38 Biplane, Naval Wing number 34. The biplane arrived at Eastchurch on 10 May 1913. Locally made 'bomb-dropping gear' was installed in November, 'sighting arrangement' added in December, the nacelle was covered with Cellon transparent sheet in February 1914 (presumably to make sighting easier), the bombing gear was removed in April 1914, dual controls fitted in September, and the aircraft delisted in February 1915.

Crashes were frequent; many aircraft were worn and torn beyond repair; aircraft were ordered, delivered, then found to be unsatisfactory after testing; and some never even got that far.

For instance, the Grahame-White Biplane bought for the army in April 1913 flew for only ten minutes before being dismissed as inadequate. The man responsible for such purchases, normally at around £1,000 per plane (about £85,000 equivalent as we write, or the price of an up-market sports car) was the Secretary of State for War, Colonel Jack Seely, noted for his soldierly qualities if not for his intellectual acuity. Introducing the Army Estimates in Parliament at this time, he stated that the Military Wing had 161 aircraft in its possession, when a realistic estimate would have been less than 50.

When Captain Patrick Hamilton joined the RFC in May 1912, he brought his own Deperdussin Monoplane with him and sold it to Jack Seely's War Office, who assigned it to No. 3 Squadron at Larkhill a few days before imposing the monoplane ban. The Donnet-Lévêque Flying Boat, with the Naval Wing at Eastchurch in October 1912, had a few flights before being wrecked in a gale when a tent fell on it and nobody thought it worth repairing.

The main machine in the Military Wing, the BE2, Blériot Experimental 2, was named for the Channel crosser because it was a tractor design rather than a Farman-style pusher. It was a wing-warper biplane, designed by Messrs de Havilland and Green at the Royal Aircraft Factory as a steady workhorse, although it never was very stable in flight until much later with the C version, which had ailerons. In any case, little pre-war thought was given to what might happen if it was attacked in the air, and a similar amount of consideration was devoted to the notion of an aircraft in the Military Wing that might be able to fight.

Of those 200 multi-various machines listed on the army side of things in the time leading up to the First World War, only two were ever fitted with an experimental gun. One was a Farman F20 of No. 3 Squadron, a pusher and a slightly more sophisticated version of the Farman Shorthorn. This was in May 1913, and it was an individual enterprise, by Lieutenant Thomas O'Brien Hubbard, later Major Hubbard MC, AFC, commanding officer of 11 Squadron and 44 Squadron, and already co-author in 1911 of *The Aeroplane*, 'an elementary text-book of the principles of dynamic flight'.

Hubbard had the observer and pilot cockpits swapped around, pilot now behind, observer to the front with a Vickers machine gun. In a pusher aircraft, of course, you couldn't fire to the rear in case you shot off your own propeller, which might not have worried the officers of No. 3 as nobody had yet imagined being swooped on from behind by a much faster German with a machine gun firing right through his own propeller. Anyway, Hubbard's experiment went no further except for one more try, some time in late 1913 or early 1914, in another Farman F20. It is not recorded if the gun was ever removed from this RFC aeroplane no. 284, and it was on No. 3 Squadron's strength at the outbreak of war, but it didn't go to France with the squadron and crashed at home shortly afterwards. Hubbard's old kite no. 352 did go, without gun, and was wrecked there a month later.

In contrast to the Military Wing, whose purpose was to serve the needs of the army as then perceived, which is to say reconnaissance, the navy boys were much more

The Henri Farman F20 with its 80hp engine could manage 70mph in the most favourable conditions but, with the weight of pilot, observer and machine gun, it was seriously underpowered.

actively engaged in experimental aggression. Naturally they had thoughts of attacking ships, and of conveying aircraft on ships so that they might get nearer to their enemy. Among the many problems here was the inability of early aircraft, fitted with floats, to withstand anything other than a calm sea. Although the American Eugene Burton Ely had taken off from a ship and landed on one, he hadn't done so while the ship was under way, and a stationary warship is not to be allowed except in harbour. The feat was achieved by Lieutenant Charles Rumney Samson (later Air Commodore RAF) on 9 May 1912, when he flew Naval Wing Aeroplane No. 2, a Short S38, from the battleship HMS *Hibernia* moving at five knots.

Lieutenant Samson in a front-elevator, Wright/Farman style pusher, flies into the record books from the decks of HMS Hibernia.

As a major role for the Naval Wing was defence of the homeland against aerial assault, they also had to think about how they might deal with enemy aircraft, in particular the Zeppelin airship. The problem was the height airships could reach, many thousands of feet beyond the capabilities of the navy's little machines, but, nothing daunted, they had a go. Aircraft number 10, a Short biplane first flown in April 1912, later fitted with floats, had a Maxim/Vickers machine gun mounted in the observer's cockpit in January 1913, but it never flew in anger. It did set something of a local record, being timed at 70mph powered by a 140hp Gnôme.

Around this time, Royal Navy intelligence must have heard about the first instance in the world of naval air power at work in war. Winched overboard from

Never doubt the courage of the Greeks. In February 1913, two of them flew one of these, a Maurice Farman Seaplane (MF7), over the Turkish fleet in the Dardanelles, which was the first instance of a fleet air arm going to war. They had to land in the sea coming back.

the Greek destroyer *Velos*, First Lieutenant Michael Moutoussis and Ensign Aristeidis Moraitinis flew their Maurice Farman seaplane over the Turkish fleet in the Dardanelles, dropped four bombs without hitting anything, and mapped the enemy's positions. We cannot know if such news had any influence, but more 'bomb-dropping gear' was installed in a Short S38 in early May 1913, at Eastchurch. Over the next few months, this particular machine seems to have been the focus of navy bombing experiments as the equipment was modified many times and developed as 'automatic bomb-dropping gear' by January 1914.

Quite how automatic it was we cannot ascertain, but this aircraft never went to war, being blown over by a gale, rebuilt, crashed, repaired, crashed again, repaired again and finally delisted in 1916.

Following the Greeks, several Maurice Farman seaplanes joined the British navy in 1913 and one of them, on 24 September of that year, was flown in 'experiments in shooting at aerial targets'. The weapon used is not specified, but if it was a rifle then the observer was a jolly good shot. Aiming at fast-moving targets from a platform swaying in every direction, he downed two wild duck.

If the Royal Naval Air Service, as it became on 1 July 1914, was to sink an enemy ship from the air, it wasn't going to do it Greek style, with bombs a man could hold in one hand. It would have to be by torpedo, and on 28 July Lieutenant A M Longmore, one of the original four naval officers accepted for pilot training back in 1911, later Air Chief Marshal Sir Arthur Murray Longmore GCB, DSO, made the first ever successful torpedo drop.

The poor weight-lifting abilities of contemporary aircraft meant that such operations could only be mounted in perfect flying weather on calm waters, and then only a shortish flight could be expected. Although more successful drops were made from a Sopwith seaplane with a 200hp engine during the first days of the war, flying slow, low and steady against a warship would have been suicide, even if you did get near enough to hope for a hit. (The RNAS would have the world's first airborne torpedo sinking a year later, in August 1915, a Turkish supply ship, from a new type of Short seaplane designed for the job.)

We must not forget how novel all this was. Without any definitive success, bombing and torpedo experiments had provided much useful experience and information, but what about gunnery? The Short company was asked to build an especially strong and powerful seaplane that could carry a heavy (by their standards) gun, and the first flights with one such were in July 1914, carrying a Vickers quick-firer, a pom-pom. Pom-poms, so called because that's what they sounded like, were light automatic cannons firing small shells very fast, and they were an infantry weapon from the Boer War made by the famous firm of Maxim, later taken over by Vickers. They were adapted as not very successful anti-aircraft guns, and here was the navy with an airborne example, a one-and-a-half pounder (shells weighing 1lb 8oz).

Tests must have been inconclusive as they were not carried on beyond the end of the year. The same aircraft would be employed later, in April 1915, to test another novelty, the Davis six-pounder, possibly effective against the dreaded Zeppelin. It was a recoilless cannon designed by an American naval officer, Cleland Davis, the no-recoil idea being specifically for aircraft, so a wood-and-cloth kite could fire such a shell, and it was achieved in a quite remarkable way.

The Davis gun was, in fact, two guns, firing in opposite directions, connected in one long barrel. As the shell came out of the business end, a charge of the same weight, made up of lead shot and grease, fired out of the other, thus cancelling out the recoil. Obviously a deal of care had to be maintained when aiming. Despite high hopes, it never really caught on.

The Davis double-firing cannon often had a third gun on top, a machine gun that the observer could use to get his aim right before releasing the six-pounder. One could argue that this tracer idea was way ahead of its time.

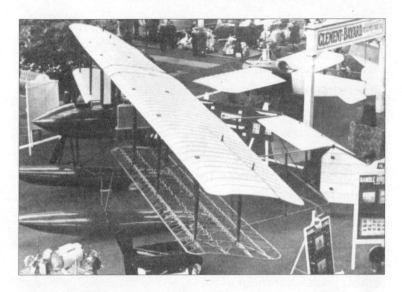

Aircraft makers often developed from firms in allied engineering businesses, such as motor cars. Hamble River Luke & Co was formed in 1912 when yacht builders Luke & Co co-operated with racing motor-boat firm Hamble River Engineering to design a seaplane. They produced a very handsome two-seater pusher, with streamlined floats and fuselage, supplied with clinker-built dinghy. The Admiralty ordered one, here pictured part-built at the 1914 Olympia Aero Show. Despite its 60-foot wingspan and 160hp engine, because it was built to the traditional quality standards of an Edwardian luxury yacht, it partly sank on launching and, even with conventional floats, never would fly.

The most far-sighted of all naval airwar initiatives started 19 November 1912, when the Admiralty ordered a gun-carrying biplane, that is, an aircraft designed to shoot down other aircraft. Varously designated the Vickers Type 18, the Vickers Destroyer and the EFB1 (Experimental Fighting Biplane No. 1), it was a pusher, so that the observer could sit at the front with a .303in machine gun and a free field of fire. It was displayed at the London air show in February 1913, a revelation that turned out to be a little premature. It probably would have flown reasonably well without the observer and the gun, but the extra weight proved too much and it nose-dived as soon as it took off, and somersaulted.

Developments through EFB2, EFB3 (with ailerons rather than wing-warping), and EFB4 led to the FB5, no longer with an E for experimental and with a 70mph top speed, the Vickers Fighting Biplane Mark 5, known as The Gunbus. The RFC career of this impressive aircraft is mainly dealt with later in this book (see 'Mr T A Terson and the Hole in his Garden'), but the one and only version of it to be put into service before the war was Naval Wing Aircraft No. 32. It never saw any action and, not being quite a production FB5 but an EFB5 (experimental prototype development of EFB3, see picture) it was struck off in March 1915.

No. 32 had a Vickers belt-fed machine gun with another Vickers device fitted, a parallel-motion gunsight, a rather complex arrangement made especially for this aircraft,

This Vickers gun carrier is an EFB5, non-production model, with a different tail arrangement, extra fin above the tailplane, but otherwise an FB5 to all intents and purposes.

which was raised and lowered automatically as the gun was aimed.

And so to war without a fighter plane. As we shall see, a few of these original and motley 400 did operate during the war and did famous things. Some even lasted into 1916 although, like the spade that had a new handle and then a new blade, and maybe another new handle, we cannot know if there was anything left of the original beyond its number.

PART TWO

There's a First Time for Everything

LOUIS STRANGE AND HIS MANY FIRSTS

By August 1914 and the outbreak of hostilities, *L'Aéronautique Militaire* was the leader in strength and technology, with at least 132 machines in 21 *escadrilles* (squadrons). Precise figures are not available but, altogether, about 400 aeroplanes were operational militarily in mainland Europe, roughly half on each side.

The RFC, Nos 2, 3, 4 and 5 Squadrons, flew 60 or so aircraft to France as part of the British Expeditionary Force, and had another 50 at home. Some RFC machines were French-designed and made, Blériot monoplanes and various Farman types including the MF7 Longhorn and the MF11 Shorthorn (basically the MF7 with the elevator on the tailplane rather than out front), plus the Avro 504 and the Royal Aircraft Factory BE2A (production model of the BE2), and the BE8. The Belgians had four escadrilles of Farmans.

The Blériot Experimental 8, called Blériot simply because it was a tractor rather than a Farman-type pusher, was a wing-warping, general-purpose, 70mph pre-war design, typical of 1914 original equipment and soon rendered obsolete. The 1915 version, BE8A, had ailerons but didn't go any faster, and was succeeded by the Avro 504, which it closely resembles.

It is easy to forget just how primitive these flying machines were. Thoughts of First World War aircraft tend to bring forth images of the famous fighters from the later years, the Sopwith Camel, the SE5A, the Fokker Triplane of Baron von Richthofen. Those neat, fast, manoeuvrable, relatively reliable machines were technically as far away from the Farman Longhorn, aka the mechanical cow, as they themselves were from the Spitfire.

On 4 November 1914, three RFC Farman Shorthorns left the UK to fly to Egypt, to support the Indian Army guarding the Suez Canal. They got there on 17 November.

The BE2A, for instance, had a 70hp Renault engine and could manage around 75mph, although ground speed would be a lot less against the wind. Its ceiling was just 10,000 feet and it could take nearly an hour to get there.

Much encouraged by First Lord of the Admiralty Churchill, was the RFC Naval Wing, now split off as the Royal Naval Air Service, with about forty 'normal' aircraft, of which one squadron was soon in France, and another fifty or so seaplanes (hydro-aeroplanes). There were no aircraft carriers of course; seaplanes took off from modified merchant ships or were lowered into the water. In either case they had to land in the sea and be hauled back aboard. Initially, the main role of the RNAS was keeping watch around the home coast for possible attacks by the German navy and, less likely, airforce.

Despite the navy's armed experiments, all of these aircraft were tools of reconnaissance and nothing more. Flights of 50 miles into enemy territory could be made, but there was very little thought of them doing any actual fighting. Surprisingly perhaps, aircraft's value in directing artillery fire had not been deeply considered, surprising until we remember to ask how aircrew were supposed to communicate with guncrew.

Aircraft, it was understood, would be able to observe and operate where the cavalry could not, to espy enemy positions and numbers. The pilot would report to HQ on landing or, where matters were more pressing, write a note as he was flying along and drop it attached to a weight where he hoped someone might pick it up.

There were no fighter aircraft yet in service. On the first day of war, no French, Belgian or German aircraft was armed at all. Guns were not in the specification although, as we have seen, the idea had been tried out. Perhaps it was a question of priorities, the chief one being to fly reliably. In 1913, it was extremely difficult to keep aero-engines going for more than an hour.

In August 1914, if enemies were to come across each other in the air, the pilots had their service revolvers and, in the two-seaters, the observers had rifles. They might also carry hand-grenades in little wooden racks in the cockpit, for dropping on anything passing below. There were no bombs to be had.

The situation was the same on both sides and, depending on the longevity of aircraft type, some of it lasted years. Manfred von Richthofen, eventually attributed 80 kills, would begin his flying career in late 1915 as an observer armed with a rifle and, at first, he thought this a reasonable idea, he being an ex-cavalry officer and (therefore) a good shot.

That was the status quo as Germany invaded Belgium on 3 August. Aeroplanes were a substitute for cavalry as scouts; the need for them to be armed was not widely comprehended; and messages from them could be passed on to HQ when and if the opportunity arose.

Like 3 Squadron's Lieutenant Hubbard more than a year earlier, Lieutenant Louis Arbon Strange of No. 5 Squadron RFC was a man of independent thought and he believed he had a contribution to make. He was one of the founding members of The Upside Down Club (pilots who had looped the loop) and was always entering races and pushing aircraft to their limits.

As the war began, as far as we know only one aircraft, a Farman pusher, also probably an F20 like Hubbard's, was fitted with a weapon, a machine gun strapped to the side of the fuselage, and that was done by Louis Strange.

It was almost three weeks before he had a chance to try it. With the gun, ammunition and an observer, Lieutenant Penn-Gaskell, as air gunner, Strange took off in pursuit of an enemy aircraft sighted overhead. This is widely accepted as occurring on 22 August 1914, which makes it the first ever 'scramble'. Six RFC machines went up with grenades, hoping to drop them on the German, while Strange, with Penn-Gaskell ready to fire the gun, couldn't get his overloaded Farman aircraft above 3,500 feet and so had to watch the enemy fly away.

One story has a sudden manoeuvre by Strange causing Penn-Gaskell to fall out of his cockpit, but grabbing hold of something as he went and, with Strange's help, regaining safety. There is a very similar, later incident featuring Strange himself, alone in an aircraft that flipped over. The man tells this in his own memoir (see below) but doesn't mention anything about Penn-Gaskell, so we can probably conclude that the earlier observer version was a bit of an aerial folktale. In any case, on their return, their commanding officer ordered Strange to cease his gun experiments.

Squadron Commander Leslie da Costa Penn-Gaskell would be killed in action on 4 February 1916, aged thirty-four.

Louis Strange had another first, when he recorded the successful destruction of enemy goods by an aircraft, using his home-made petrol bomb to set fire to two German trucks on 28 August.

By October 1914, the pusher Farmans in No. 5 Squadron had been replaced by the 80mph tractor Avro 504, which presented the opposite gunning problem. A gun in a pusher could fire forwards but not back; a gun in a tractor aircraft could fire back, hopefully missing the tail, good for defence but not much use for attack. Strange devised a sling for a Lewis gun to hang from the upper wing, and a harness for the observer so he could stand up and fire forwards, over the pilot's head and over the propeller.

To modern eyes, the Avro 504 looks like something a child would produce when asked to draw a biplane, but Louis Strange flew at the enemy in one.

Presumably with his CO's permission, on 22 November 1914 Strange and his observer Lieutenant F G Small scored the first British victory by an aircraft with a fitted gun, although not shooting the enemy down with it. They forced an enemy plane, variously given as an Albatros or an Aviatik, to the ground behind Entente lines near the Belgian border. Small had been wounded in the fight so Strange flew back to base, leaving the army below to take the German aviators prisoner, which must have been quite a wrench for poor Louis, being unable to meet his very own Huns.

On 26 March 1915 the *London Gazette* announced the award of the Military Cross to Second Lieutenant (temporary Captain) L A Strange: 'For gallantry and ability on reconnaissance and other duties on numerous occasions, especially on the occasion when he dropped three bombs from a height of only 200 feet on the railway junction at Courtrai, whilst being assailed by heavy rifle fire.'

Dropping bombs by hand was restrictive. You could only drop one at a time and you might not want to keep passing low right over a specific target again and again, so Strange contrived a bomb-release mechanism. Four twenty-pounders on racks under the wings could be dropped by yanking on a wire in the cockpit. It was simple but new. As there was no method of priming/ fusing the bombs in the air, Strange must have flown with bombs at the ready, knowing that if he crashed, or was hit by ground fire, the whole lot could go up. He certainly proved his point at Courtrai on 10 March, when he closed the station for days and caused many casualties.

His most acrobatic feat occurred in May 1915, when he fitted a Lewis gun to the top wing. To reload, he had to stand up in the cockpit; the aircraft flipped over on to its back, with Louis hanging on to the upper wing and somehow managing to steer the thing with his feet:

'I kept on kicking upwards behind me until at last I got one foot and then the other hooked inside the cockpit. Somehow I got the stick between my legs again, and jammed on full aileron and elevator; I do not know exactly what happened then, but the trick was done. The machine came over the right way up, and I fell off the top plane and into my seat with a bump.'

Strange continued to innovate right through the war, in gunnery, bombing and tactics, and finished as Lieutenant-Colonel, DSO, MC, DFC, commanding a fighter wing of seven squadrons. 'Finished' is the wrong word, because he joined the RAF Volunteer Reserve at the age of fifty and went back to France in the Second World War and had a distinguished new career as an operations commander. He died in 1966.

HERBERT MUSGRAVE AND HIS FLYING WIRELESS

It only took a few weeks of the war for the combatants to realise that several new uses of aircraft were desirable and, as Bertram Dickson had predicted, the more valuable aircraft became, the more pressing became the need to stop them working. Anti-aircraft artillery ('archie') didn't seem to be very effective. Where were the fighter planes? There were none, yet.

Archie, incidentally, was a nickname said to derive from a certain pilot's habit of singing the chorus from a George Robey music-hall song, 'Archibald, Certainly Not!', as he noted the German gunners' inability to explode their shells at the correct height. The pilot in question, Captain Amyas Borton, ex-Black Watch, later Air Vice-Marshal RAF, was a flight commander at 5 Squadron, a well-known figure in the small RFC community, so such a coining is perfectly feasible. Later in the war, when the German anti-aircraft gunners became rather better at their trade, the name stuck although the humour was long gone out of it.

Flights over roads crowded with troops and equipment showed obvious targets. The mechanics of No. 4 Squadron fitted Lewis guns to two newly arrived Shorthorns in September 1914 and one of them performed the first strafing, of a German column on the road, firing 250 rounds on 31 October 1914. Hand-dropped grenades did little damage. Big, proper bombs would be good, but there were none of those either, and no means of carrying them, or aiming them accurately, had been devised.

Photographs would be good too, for analysis at HQ, and the limitations of leaning over the side of the aircraft with a press camera made clear the requirement for a purpose-made system fixed to the aircraft and a mobile laboratory to develop the pictures.

The greatest eye-opener was the new message technology, the wireless telegraph, and the RFC had the only two military aircraft fitted with it.

There had been ad hoc experiments with wireless in aircraft from the RFC's earliest days, mostly by the Naval Wing, but there hadn't been a really co-ordinated effort until April 1914, when a few aircraft and officers had been placed at the disposal of Captain (acting Major) Herbert Musgrave of the Royal Engineers, a decorated Boer War veteran. His father, Sir Anthony, had been colonial governor of Jamaica, Newfoundland and Queensland and had had towns, streets and mountains named after him.

Herbert Musgrave's brief was technical. The standard procedure to this point had been for scientific experiments to be conducted by the National Physical Laboratory, the results of which were then passed down the line for the aviators to try out. With war looking more and more likely, and with the suspicion that the boffins at the lab were not necessarily thinking about the things that most concerned fighting men, Musgrave was told to speed up matters. As OC The Experimental Branch of the Military Wing, Royal Flying Corps, he was sent to the curiously named 'Concentration Camp', Netheravon, which was a kind of grand exercise for all four squadrons in response to the distant thunderings of a possible European war. Musgrave was to conduct trials in ballooning, kiting, photography, meteorology, bomb-dropping, musketry, gunnery, artillery co-operation, and communications.

Musgrave, to his credit, didn't bother too much about muskets and kites but concentrated on communications and the miracle of wireless.

Royal Aircraft Factory BE2A machines of No. 2 Squadron line up beside the tents at Netheravon, June 1914.

Wireless had been carried in airships since at least 1912. Airships could cope with the weight but flimsy little aeroplanes struggled with the massive sets available at the time. Certainly there was no possibility of carrying a wireless set and an observer.

Herbert Musgrave, Boer War hero and wireless visionary.

On his staff, Musgrave had pilots Lieutenant Donald Swain Lewis, late of No. 2 Squadron, and Lieutenant Baron Trevenen James, Royal Engineers. They made a trip in June 1914 of thirty miles, flying ten miles apart, communicating wirelessly by Morse code all the way. What use that might be entirely escaped the generals.

Events overtook Musgrave. Lewis and James were transferred to No. 4 Squadron and to France on 13 August

1914. They were the squadron's wireless section, not thought to be especially important and, at first, the only aeroplane-borne military wireless in the world could do little to change that view. Equipment was lacking and no more could be had. Wireless only worked if there were ground stations not too far away, but the Entente powers were in retreat and none could be properly established.

The usual method was to carry the 'portable' wireless ground-station in two horse-drawn wagons, in the charge of its chief mechanic, Sergeant Ellison, known as Fonso, and set it up wherever the RFC was going to stay for more than a day. The arrival of Fonso's Circus thus informed the men that they probably were not going to move on again, until tomorrow anyway.

Hardly surprisingly, considering there were only two aerial wireless sets, the first major contribution to the war from aerial reconnaissance was by conventional methods. The RFC flew twelve 'recco' sorties on 22 August. One reported that von Kluck's army, on the right flank of the German advance through Belgium, seemed to be preparing to turn the left flank of the British position at Mons and possibly surround the British Expeditionary Force. The reporters were Captain L E O Charlton and Lieutenant V H N Wadham, who landed and passed on their intelligence by telephone, and it was quite different to what the cavalry was saying. The High Command listened to the report and started a withdrawal, averting a potential disaster. One up for the fly boys.

Captain Vivian Hugh Nicholas Wadham would be killed in January 1916. Charlton would survive.

Four days later, on 26 August, with the Entente armies

now retreating from Mons, Lieutenant Lewis set out from St Quentin in his BE2A fitted with wireless. The set filled the observer's cockpit.

Lewis was to follow a Farman aircraft of No. 5 Squadron, which was to land at Landrecies, in the Nord department, where there had been a fight the day before between British Army I Corps and the German Fifth Army. The 5 Squadron pilot was to signal by lamp the current position of I Corps' headquarters, and Lewis was to pass the information to staff officers by wireless.

The Farman landed but no signal was forthcoming. Lewis circled for an hour under fire but had to give up, short on fuel and with his machine damaged by shells and rifle bullets. So far, no good but, come 6 September, the official opening day of the Battle of the Marne (there had been some fighting there the day before), Lewis was again working with I Corps.

He set out from St Quentin in his BE2A, as von Kluck wheeled his First Army to meet the attacking French and British, opening a gap between his own forces and the German Second Army. At its widest, this gap in the enemy lines was thirty miles or so. Lewis saw it, and sent a wireless message reporting his observations. The response was immediate, with British commanders sending their troops to join the French in charging through the gap.

This is the first record of a wireless message being sent on active service from a British aeroplane, to be received and acted upon, and so is the first record of its kind altogether. Its significance was deeply appreciated. With one transmission, Lieutenant Lewis had changed the opinion of hundreds of generals on both sides of the war and made immediately necessary the introduction of fighter aircraft. From the German point of view, Lewis and his ilk had to be stopped.

It was a small step from reporting on troops and enemy installations to the idea of target marking with wireless. You fire your artillery, I'll tell you where your shells are landing, you alter your aim accordingly. All very well, but the pilot was alone with his heavy, inanimate passenger and had to transmit Morse while flying his aircraft, which was a full-time occupation in itself, with constant adjustments having to be made to keep the frail machine where the pilot wanted to be and meanwhile being shot at. It was just as well that his wireless set could not receive, so there were no questions or instructions from the ground.

At first, the pilot's messages were what you might expect, up a bit, left a bit, hit, hit, hit. By October 1914, maps with grid references would be in use, and codes devised so that a few Morse letters and numbers could indicate so many yards to the west, north or whatever of the bullseye.

As was often the way, progress was made because of the vision and determination of a few individual officers. In between original thinking and organisation to cope with a set of problems nobody had confronted before, and flying on operations, Lewis and James would go to Paris to buy wireless kit.

During the first Battle of the Aisne, starting on 13 September as the Germans, retreating from the first Marne battle, turned to face the Entente powers and thus begin four years of almost immobile trench warfare, stability of positions meant that it was at last possible to organise fixed ground stations for wireless.

After initial scepticism at messages arriving by Morse rather than horse, the artillery grew to love it. By 27 September, the RFC formed a Headquarters Wireless Unit at Fère-en-Tardenois, in Picardie, with Major Musgrave in charge. Growth was the intention. The demand for this kind of air co-operation already vastly exceeded the supply.

'Today,' said General Sir Horace Smith-Dorrien in a telegram to GHQ dated 27 September:

> I watched for a long time an aeroplane observing for the 6-inch howitzers of the 3rd Division. It was, at times, smothered with hostile anti-aircraft guns, but nothing daunted, it continued for hours through a wireless installation to observe the fire and, indeed, to control the battery with most satisfactory results. I am not mentioning names as to do so, where all are daily showing such heroic and efficient work, would be invidious.

Invidious indeed, but it was probably Lewis or James. The ideal artillery spotter was a stationary one, the better to report accurately as firing progressed, which was why balloons had been favoured and would remain in use for some time. Balloons were much employed by the Germans; they could be wound down rapidly as aerial danger approached and, later, the crew could jump with parachutes. For the moment, Lewis and James made nice targets for the enemy, with no parachutes.

General Smith-Dorrien was deeply impressed but to most of those on the ground, it was all in a day's work. According to a Royal Engineers officer in the trenches, by the autumn of 1914 aeroplanes had ceased being a novelty and attacks on them and by them held little interest. He wrote:

> We see aeroplanes nearly every day and generally they are being shelled. The aeroplane is surrounded by little puffs of white smoke, usually at a slightly lower level than the aeroplane itself. Each puff represents the burst of a shrapnel shell. Although I have seen at least a dozen of these performances, I have never seen an aeroplane brought down. Apparently it is awfully difficult for the gunners to get the range of an object in the air, and in any case that object is moving very rapidly. There is an anti-aircraft section of the artillery, armed, I believe, with a sort of pom-pom which fires little one inch shells in rapid succession.

This officer was clearly not familiar with the Maxim (later Vickers) light automatic cannon, similar to the one experimentally carried by the Short seaplane pre-war. This one fired a 37mm (approximately 1.5-inch) shell weighing a pound but it was not very successful. Unless the gunners had their range perfectly calculated, any shells that hit went straight through aircraft plywood and fabric. Our engineer continues:

The French and Belgian aeroplanes throw out little pencil-shaped rods, which will kill a man if they strike him on the head but I don't think these projectiles cause much damage, and the Germans don't use them. The chief use of aeroplanes is to direct the fire of the artillery.

The men have got so used to seeing aeroplanes shelled fruitlessly that the sight of one scarcely attracts a look. At first they all used to stop work to watch the show; now they murmur something about 'another blooming aeroplane' and take no further notice.

When the ninth squadron of the Royal Flying Corps was formed on 8 December 1914 at St Omer, the CO was the British army's most enthusiastic and successful wireless man, Herbert Musgrave, and among his officers were Lewis and James, now captains, commanding 'B' and 'A' Flights respectively. Not surprisingly, wireless was top priority in the new squadron.

To start with, No. 9 Squadron's main aircraft type was the BE2A, but there were Blériot 11 monoplanes too, and Farman Longhorns and Shorthorns. Fitting these with continuously redesigned wireless sets of at least three different basic types was a challenge to be met by a very scarce resource, trained wireless mechanics. The few there were, worked under canvas and slept in barns, trying to fit in some training of others while meeting the non-stop demands of the artillery and wishing some help would turn up soon.

The pressures of war forced rapid development of wireless

sets, which soon shrunk to make room for an observer again who, from above enemy positions with a pilot concentrating entirely on flying, could send comprehensive information to his fellow soldiers on the ground.

The British Army commanders were now evangelists for wireless and decided that all their squadrons should have wireless flights, and so No. 9 became the supply centre. As flights were formed, trained and equipped, they were sent off to other squadrons until there was one left, C1 Flight, flying Shorthorns under the direction of Captain Hugh Caswell Tremenheere Dowding, later Air Chief Marshal Lord Dowding GCB, GCVO, CMG, head of Fighter Command in the Battle of Britain.

That flight was transferred to 16 Squadron on 22 March. Musgrave passed command to Dowding who went back to England with half a dozen men to Brooklands on 1 April 1915, where No. 9 became the de facto wireless school of the RFC.

Individual officers and extempore methods were still the routes to progress. Among the wireless contingent of the Cumberland and Westmorland Yeomanry, seconded to 9 Squadron, was Lieutenant Prince, who deeply impressed his CO, first by acquiring large quantities of wireless components from non-military sources, and then by devising an airborne wireless telephone. Dowding was thus the first man to receive the spoken word transmitted from a mobile phone in the air.

In the autumn of 1915, the wireless school reformed into a front-line squadron and went off to France, just in time to meet Hauptmann Oswald Boelcke, the first fighter ace to reach double figures, and his competitive colleague,

Leutnant Max Immelmann. They were flying the world's first really effective fighter aircraft, the Fokker Eindecker. But that's another story.

The heroic and efficient James and Lewis flew many more bloomin' aeroplanes but were destined not to last the war. Captain Baron Trevenen James MC, by then of No. 6 Squadron, was killed over Verlorenhoek, midway between Ypres and Zonnebeke, by a direct hit while observing for the artillery, on July 13 1915. His CO reported:

> [Captain James] was observing from the aeroplane alone as he generally did. He was ranging a battery and was being heavily shelled. His machine was hit by a shell and was seen to dive to the ground from a great height. The Germans dropped a note from one of their machines saying that he was dead when he fell. He met the end I am sure he would have wished for – if it had to be – suddenly, alone, and doing his duty.

Another officer noted in his diary: 'Lewis came in from spotting with his machine shot full of holes. I believe he likes it.' In February 1916, Lieutenant-Colonel Donald Swain Lewis DSO, OC Second Wing RFC, was co-operating with the Second Army in the Ypres Salient, flying a Morane Parasol east of Wytschaete, with Captain Arthur Witherby Gale DSO, 2nd Life Guards, OC 3rd Division Trench Mortars, as passenger. The aircraft was brought down by a direct hit from anti-aircraft guns and both men were killed.

Major Herbert Musgrave was awarded the DSO and went

back to the Royal Engineers, where he served as Deputy Assistant Quartermaster General. He was killed in action, aged forty-two, in June 1918.

REGINALD MARIX AND THE RIGHT BUILDING

A squadron of the Royal Naval Air Service, No. 3, arrived in France at the end of August 1914, mainly to bolster the RFC rather than to fulfil naval duties. Then No. 2 Squadron RNAS set up at Antwerp and attempted a truly daring venture on 22 September, when four aircraft were sent to the Zeppelin sheds at Düsseldorf and Cologne.

One was a Sopwith two-seater (side by side) flown by Lieutenant-Commander Spenser Grey, who had previously taken Winston Churchill for three private spins in it. In the manner of the period, it had been rebuilt after a crash and sent to Antwerp with an extra fuel tank and that 'bomb-dropping gear'. Spenser Grey headed for Cologne but didn't get there due to bad weather. One did make it through, a Sopwith Tabloid flown by Lieutenant C H Collet. After coming down through thick mist, he dropped three twenty-pounders on the shed at Düsseldorf; the two that hit the target proved to be duds.

The second attempt was, eventually, a triumph, on 8 October, by which time the squadron had withdrawn to Dunkirk. Squadron CO Spenser Grey again headed for Cologne, in a Sopwith Tabloid this time, but missed the Zeppelin base there and bombed the railway station instead. Low on fuel on the way home, he had to abandon the aircraft at Antwerp that evening. The city surrendered to the Germans on the following day.

Meanwhile, the navy's two other Sopwith Tabloids (bought by the Admiralty from the RFC) flew to attack the same sheds, one to Cologne, one to Düsseldorf.

This was a remarkable op for a number of reasons. For a start, the aircraft had been built in 1913 for the civilian market, as the aerial equivalent of a sports car. It could do 90mph, far more than standard service aircraft. A float-plane adaptation of it had won the second Schneider Trophy race in the April, at just under 87mph (the first race, in 1913, had been won at 45mph). It was said that after seeing the Tabloid in practice, most of the other competitors didn't bother racing.

The RNAS pilots were in the single-seater version, unarmed at this point in the war, flying alone right into the Fatherland, with nothing more than their service revolvers. It was a sensation. Here is an eye-witness report:

I was in Düsseldorf when the English airman visited the town for the second time. It was a splendid feat, he took the Germans by surprise. The soldiers seeing the hostile aircraft high up in the air shot at it continually until suddenly the aeroplane started to glide lower and lower; the people were mad with joy and shouted hurrah. The soldiers got ready to catch the aeroplane as it fell when suddenly from a height of between 100 and 200 metres the airman threw several bombs, one of which reached its goal, the Zeppelin shed, in which there was the air-cruiser, the pride of Düsseldorf, which had received orders to join the army in France that afternoon. In spite of my

being a good distance away, I heard the explosion,
the smoke whirling high into the air, and I saw
the airman escape in the common confusion.

The German papers next day had 'Zeppelin shed slightly damaged' and failed to mention the four army officers killed or the heap of ashes that was the remains of airship Z9.

The English airman was Lieutenant Reginald L G Marix. While his aircraft was being hit five times by rifle shots and *mitrailleuse* (a multi-barrelled machine gun, like the Gatling), he dropped two twenty-pounders from less than 600 feet and changed the military outlook on bombing. As *The Times* said: 'There has always been a little uncertainty about the value of bomb-dropping, for although it seemed possible that buildings might be set alight with incendiary explosives, it was another matter to make sure of hitting the right building. The naval pilots have now shown at Düsseldorf that this is possible.'

Marix and Collet were both awarded the DSO; Spenser-Grey already had one.

The Admiralty pointed out that the importance of the Collet attack lay in the fact that it showed, 'in the event of further bombs being dropped into Antwerp and other Belgian towns, measures of reprisal can certainly be adopted, if desired, to almost any extent'.

The Times added a footnote: 'Demand for air risk insurance. There was again a very large amount of insurance effected in London yesterday against the risks of damage by aircraft and bombs and shells thrown therefrom; and underwriters hardened their rates. A premium of 2s 6d per cent is now regarded as the minimum.'

Lieutenant Cyril Gordon Hosking and Captain Theodore Crean of RFC No. 4 Squadron were the victims of another first on 26 October when their BE2A, was shot down by the British Army at Poperinghe. The Germans also shot at their own aircraft. According to Manfred von Richthofen, later the Red Baron but on the ground around this time, he and his fellow soldiers were not even aware that aircraft carried markings to distinguish their nationalities, still less did they know one aircraft type from another. So they usually shot at any aircraft they saw.

Captain Charles Herbert Collet DSO was killed in a flying accident at Imbros on 19 August 1915.

THE FIRST SKIRMISHES AND GILBERT MAPPLEBECK

On 19 August 1914, Captain Philip Joubert de la Ferté, (later Air Chief Marshal KCB, CMG, DSO), in a Blériot of No. 3 Squadron RFC, and Lieutenant Gilbert William Mapplebeck in a BE2A of No. 4 Squadron left Maubeuge aerodrome at 09.30 on the first RFC reconnaissance operation of the war. Both pilots got lost and had to land to ask for directions, and neither gathered any really useful gen on the whereabouts of the enemy or the Belgian allies.

Mapplebeck had established something of a reputation in the tiny, elite society of airmen. His earlier antics had included crashing a Farman on his first flight at the Central Flying School, earning an admonition from his 4 Squadron CO for looping the loop in a BE2, and flying lower than everyone else during the aerial salute at the close of the Netheravon concentration camp, threatening to frighten the horse and remove the ceremonial hat of General Smith-Dorrien.

On 22 August, an Avro 504 of No. 5 Squadron became the first RFC loss of the war in combat; several aircraft and their crews had already been lost in accidents. Second Lieutenant Vincent Waterfall, aged 23, originally of the East Yorkshires, and Lieutenant Charles George Gordon Bayly, Royal Engineers, also 23, were killed when shot down by small-arms fire over Belgium. Also on this day, Sergeant Major Jillings (later Squadron Leader Jillings MC), observer with Lieutenant Noel of No. 2 Squadron, was wounded by a rifle bullet fired by a German cavalryman, so that too was a first for the RFC.

The German army was forcing its way south towards Reims, threatening the aerodrome at Maubeuge, so 3 and 4 Squadrons withdrew twenty miles east to Le Câteau, while 2 Squadron moved to Berlaimont. Further enemy advances kept the squadrons more or less constantly on the move. Aircrew setting off on an operation hardly knew if they'd be able to come home to a field still in Entente hands, and living conditions were rough, especially for the non-officers who had to sleep where they might, sometimes under the aircraft. Officers would generally find a billet in the nearest village.

Here is James McCudden, future fighter ace and VC, now serving as a mechanic:

I found Mr Conran and his Parasol Blériot 616 in a muddy ploughed field, so I filled up with petrol and oil and had a look around the engine and machine and then tied it down for the night. It was raining very hard, and as there were six inches of mud under the machine I decided not to sleep under the wing that night, so I slept in the pilot's seat with a waterproof sheet over me.

This Mr Conran, by the way, Lieutenant E L Conran of 3 Squadron, was the man who made the first RFC bombing raid, on 24 August. He dropped one small prototype bomb aiming for three German aeroplanes on the ground. He missed.

Not only were all the aircraft of that time grossly underpowered, so that they were the playthings of the wind while flying; they could also be blown about on the ground. The hangars were tents, so they could be blown down too, and the aircraft could be soaked in heavy rain, making them even more difficult to fly, but everything was new. Almost everything they did, in one way or another had never been done before. That in itself was a great motivator.

There was another first on 26 August: a dogfight, what the Germans called *Kurvenkampf*, curving struggle/fight. Three BE2A aircraft of No. 2 Squadron took off from Le Cateau to try to catch a Taube that was nosying about, and Lieutenant Harvey-Kelly with Sergeant Major Street forced it to land, partially wrecking it but not damaging the crew, who escaped while Harvey-Kelly was landing beside his prize. If shooting the pilot with a hand-held gun didn't work, this was the only way to gain a fighter-style victory. By buffeting and generally threatening to bounce and bash, and using the turbulence caused by close approaches, it was occasionally possible to win a submission.

Major Hubert Dunsterville Harvey-Kelly DSO would be killed in action on 29 April 1917, while with 19 Squadron, a fighter squadron then flying the SPAD 7.

That was it in Le Cateau for the moment because the German army was marching into the town by that lunchtime, and the RFC moved to St Quentin for a day, before shifting again to La Fère, and again, and again, almost daily as the Entente powers retreated.

James McCudden: 'We had some lunch here in the shape of some fried bully beef, the frying being done in an opened petrol tin. We had some tea, too, but no milk, so Mr Conran rose to the occasion and milked a cow in a neighbouring field with great success.'

Lieutenant Mapplebeck, he of the first aerial recco, repeated the force-down performance on behalf of No. 4 Squadron on another Taube at Le Quesnoy, this time capturing plane and crew.

It was another month before 4 Squadron had its first casualty and, of course, it had to be Mapplebeck, the fighter pilot without a fighter. He had been detailed to destroy a German balloon by dropping bombs on it but on the way, in his BE2A, he met an enemy aircraft. To drop a bomb on this new target seemed like a good idea but, while he was coaxing his reluctant machine into a good position at 6,000 feet, the German observer shot Mapplebeck with a rifle.

It was only one round and it might not have caused much damage had it not hit a five-franc piece in his pocket. The coin and the bullet shattered and the effect was like that of a miniature nail bomb, with bits of shrapnel cutting open his thigh and stomach. In pain and losing a lot of blood, he managed to fly back into friendly territory and to come down at Dhuizel.

This effort would earn him a DSO. He was taken to a field hospital and, over several days, had nine operations to remove pieces of metal. These lines are from a letter to his mother:

> This is about the fifth day after receiving my wounds. I am getting on well and there is practically no doubt of my recovery. I am going to a place near Paris. I am not sure of its name, but will write you later. The place is Prince Murat's home. I met him sometime over here and he came to see me when he heard about me and said he would take me there. If you would like to I'm sure you can come and stay with me. I will speak to him about it.
>
> This is really only a clearing hospital where they bring the wounded only for a day at most as a rule. I was not moved because I was too bad and shall probably stay here three or four days longer. General French has been awfully kind. He even came to see me himself and generals pop in quite often to ask me how I am going on.

He recovered from his wounds and returned to duty.

The battle of Neuve Chapelle began on 10 March 1915. It was the first British offensive with the objective of breaking through German lines, and it made the most thorough use yet of aerial reconnaissance of enemy trenches. Indeed, the maps used to plan the attacks were put together from photographs and reports, although when the advance began, mist and cloud stopped aircraft from seeing much of what was going on below. As infantry had no means of communication, once the men were out of their trenches nobody could tell what was happening at all. One 9 Squadron pilot returned from a fruitless recco saying that he'd had to keep all his flying controls in constant use or they would have frozen solid.

The attack began well, and might have gone better if a new stratagem to hinder German reinforcements had worked. The novel idea was to bomb the railways that would carry the extra troops to the front, and five targets were allocated. A great many sorties were flown, almost 150, three or four aircraft at a time, going back again and again, but with very little success. The official estimate from HQ was three good results. Most of the raids were made with the newly commonplace twenty pounders, but some were quite different.

Three pilots of 4 Squadron, including Mapplebeck, were briefed to attack the railway junction at Lille, in the early hours of the second day, 11 March, a mission that would be a triple first. One, it was part of the railway stratagem, being the first organised attempt at disrupting enemy troop movements by bombing; two, each BE2 would carry a fearsome novelty load, two 100lb bombs, on experimental racks made by the squadron mechanics; three, as it meant taking off and flying to the target in the dark, they would be directed there by lights on the ground.

The trio had flown to a field at Bailleul the day before, as near as they could get to Lille and, marking the direction of a straight bombing run to the railway junction, two electric lamps were set, five miles apart, the further one a little short of the front line. One source suggests that the pilots also had flashlights with them, strapped to their backs, for communicating with each other, although what their messages might have been is not clear.

Captains Barton and Warrand and Lieutenant Mapplebeck took off at 04.45. Barton crashed almost immediately owing to a terminal combination of engine failure and extra weight, but without hurting himself. Mapplebeck also had engine trouble but managed to get back and land in the dark with his massive bomb load.

Warrand flew on and was observed passing over the nearer directing light. Everyone listened for a new sound, of a 100lb bomb exploding. Twenty minutes later they heard it, twice, but they never saw Warrand again. Captain Alastair St John Munro Warrand, initially of the Black Watch, was shot down by ground fire and, wounded, taken prisoner. As was the way on both sides, he was given the best possible medical treatment. However, he died of his wounds on 19 March, age 26.

The mechanics, unsung heroes of every air war, fixed Mapplebeck's engine and off he went again. He, too, was noted flying over the nearer light, but that was it. He was shot down, but not injured, behind enemy lines. The

Germans couldn't find him before he knocked on the door of a farmhouse and was given shelter. Later, his saviour smuggled him into Lille and took him to meet the mayor, Monsieur Jacquet, who helped him with civilian clothes and money.

Mapplebeck spoke French well and was unlikely to be discovered, but posters were put up threatening the firing squad for anyone hiding him and offering a large reward for his arrest. He left at night, walked into Holland, and was back in London in a week.

He came back to flying in France and the next time he was over Lille he dropped a note addressed to Crown Prince Rupprecht of Bavaria, commander of the German 6th Army, apologising for not being able to pay his respects during his short stay.

Meanwhile, the two days of the abortive Neuve Chapelle offensive had cost 12,000 casualties for a gain of less than one acre of land. Months later, Jacquet would be arrested, charged with aiding French and British combatants including Mapplebeck, and shot with three fellow-members of the unnamed Great War resistance.

Mapplebeck's DSO had been announced in the *London Gazette* on 18 February 1915, the same day as Major Musgrave's, and on 23 March his Bar, also the same day as Musgrave. Captain Gilbert William Mapplebeck DSO and Bar would be killed on 24 August 1915, test flying a new French monoplane, possibly a prototype of the fast, mid-wing Morane-Saulnier Type N, an advanced design but unpopular and difficult to handle, improved in later models.

ADOLPHE PÉGOUD AND HIS SIX VICTIMS

Lewis and James had flown largely unopposed while they created their new product, aerial wireless intelligence. Fire from the ground was a danger but not a compelling one. As the demand for the product rose, more and more flights were made over enemy lines by both sides. The Germans would soon catch up with wireless, so some method had to be devised on both sides for stopping those flying spies. But how could aircraft be shot down when they were out of range of small arms and seemingly unperturbed by inept anti-aircraft artillery?

The claim for the first actual air-to-air shooting down belongs to the French, but still that was not with a gun factory-fitted to the aircraft. Sergeant Joseph Frantz and his observer Corporal Louis Quénault were in a Voisin 3, a pusher, on the morning of 5 October 1914, on patrol near the village of Jonchery-sur-Vesle, Reims. They had the standard French army machine gun of the time, the 8mm Hotchkiss, which they had specially mounted behind the front cockpit on a tripod stand, so that Quénault could stand up and fire forwards over the pilot's head as Small and Strange had done.

The intrepid Frenchmen spotted an enemy machine, an Aviatik, and flew at it. As both aircraft manoeuvred and counter-manoeuvred – as far as was possible in a Voisin and an Aviatik – Quénault fired several bursts from his machine gun without downing the German, before he ran out of ammunition.

The German observer, Leutnant Fritz von Zangen, began firing on the French crew with a rifle, so Quénault picked up his rifle and shot the pilot, Sergeant Wilhelm

You have to admire these fighter boys, going up in a 60mph kite with no defence behind. Like all the aircraft that began the war, the Voisin 3 was not designed for warfare if, by 'warfare', we mean fighting, and it had not been designed to carry the weight of a machine gun. Although the Hotchkiss was reasonably reliable, it could still jam. On the ground, with the French infantry, it needed a gun crew of three to keep it going, feeding in belts of ammunition. For aerial use it was modified to take a circular magazine but in a Voisin there wasn't room for many of those.

Schlichting. The Aviatik, out of control, fell from the sky and exploded as it hit the ground.

Clearly, this state of affairs could not continue.

The first fighter ace, defined as one with five aerial victories, was also a Frenchman, Adolphe Célestin Pégoud, he who was the second man to loop the loop and the first to make a parachute jump.

Before that, he had been among the first, if not *the* first, to fly any serious distance upside down. Little was known about such a trick, so he tied himself very tightly into his seat before attempting it and, on 2 September 1913, climbed to 3,000 feet and flew for over 2,000 feet the wrong way up. Among several discoveries was the interesting fact that the petrol supply to the engine stopped when the machine was *tête en bas*, and sprayed the pilot's face instead. After that, on the same day, he did *un looping*.

He came to England, to Hendon, to perform his aerobatics, and was much in demand throughout Europe. In fact, he was on the point of embarking for America when war broke out.

He was posted to the Western Front in October 1914 and flew missions against troops and balloons, and becoming well aware of how poorly armed he was expected to be, fixed a machine gun to his aircraft for his observer to operate. In December, hit in the engine by small-arms fire from the ground, he glided his machine for 10km to regain his own lines. On 5 February 1915, flying a Farman of the 25ème Escadrille, he took credit as the pilot for his first two victories although they were actually shot down by his observer, and his third was a forced landing: one Taube and two Aviatiks in one day. His fourth and fifth victims fell on 3 April 1915, both Aviatiks, and his sixth on 11 July, another Aviatik, although Alphonse was now flying a Morane Parasol of the 49ème Escadrille.

Before the war he had been a flying instructor as well as a famous aerobatics performer. One of his pupils was a German called Walter (sometimes Otto) Kandulski, and he it was who piloted the two-seater from which Adolphe was shot down, the first ace and the first ace to be killed in action. That was on 31 August 1915, hit in the head by a stray bullet.

By this time, the first real fighter aircraft, the Fokker Eindecker, was terrorising Entente aircrew and fighter aces would soon be qualifying in large numbers. Pégoud's achievement was remarkable because he didn't have such an aircraft, just the unreliable, underpowered kites of earliest times, and his bravery was recognised with the Médaille Militaire and the Légion d'Honneur.

MR T A TERSON AND THE HOLE IN HIS GARDEN

Christmas 1914 is famous as the one when enemy soldiers climbed out of their trenches for a game of football, but it should also be famous as the first time that an aircraft designed as a fighter went into action. It was on the home front, too.

After only a few months of war, everyone recognised the notion of fighter aircraft as a separate type, ideally single-seater, fast, nippy, that could outmanoeuvre slower, less nimble enemies and give them the deadly burst. Two years previously, the Admiralty commission to Vickers to come up with a fighting aircraft had not quite resulted in that ideal because, with no other choice that they could see, the designers had gone with a two-seater pusher format.

The FB5 is usually thought to have been the first British aeroplane purpose-made to carry a gun, but there are other candidates. Sopwith produced a Gun-Carrying Seaplane, also a pusher, which was delivered to the Naval Wing sometime in the summer of 1913 with a .303 machine gun in the front cockpit; but it was not highly regarded, and neither were the gunless versions. Avro designed a twin-engined seaplane gun-carrier that was not delivered. One example of the land-based derivative of the Sopwith, the 80mph Sopwith Type 806 Gunbus (first flight October 1914), was briefly in France with the RNAS in February 1915 but there is no record of any action.

That the Vickers FB5 was the result of the first fighter-aircraft commission cannot be doubted, as the others surely came along after the Admiralty started the idea, and the ultimate distinction of the first incident of a designated fighter aircraft flying at the enemy also belongs with the Vickers FB5.

It came about because the Germans decided to bomb mainland Britain. They chose 24 December 1914 for the first unfriendly bomb ever to be dropped on British soil, and not by a Zeppelin, as everyone expected, but by hand from an aeroplane.

'British soil' were the right words on that Christmas Eve morning. At about 11am, one German craft dropped (or threw, as they usually termed it) one bomb into the vegetable garden of Mr T A Terson of Dover, making a hole ten feet wide and four feet deep, breaking windows in several nearby houses and scattering Brussels sprouts and winter cabbages everywhere. A man up a tree in the garden next door was blown from it but landed softly in some bushes. A young chap, a solicitor's son called Mowll, said he was 25 yards away talking to a friend when the bomb exploded, covering him and friend in earth.

The identity of the raider is open to some question. One source firmly suggests a navy float-plane, a Friedrichshafen FF29; civilian eye-witness accounts state equally firmly it was a Taube, looking 'like a big seagull'. In any case, it dropped its load and flew away.

Next day, Christmas Day, another raider invaded Britain, again identified in one report as a Friedrichshafen FF29 but described from the ground as an Albatros. It was spotted near Sheerness but disappeared into the clouds and fog, to emerge between Purfleet and Erith, well up the Thames, beyond where the Dartford crossing now is, triggering anti-aircraft fire from pom-pom guns on roofs and the scrambling of three RFC aircraft. This was it; the first use of a fighter.

An aerial battle of sorts ensued, as the German crew fled with only their rifle and pistols to protect them, pursued by the home team, at least one of which, according to the papers, had 'a quick-firing gun'.

That was the Vickers Gunbus, which had taken off from Joyce Green aerodrome at Dartford.

Whichever German aircraft it was, the FF29 or the Albatros, top speed was about the same at around 60mph (95kph). The FB5 Gunbus was a little faster and it caught the German up, got near enough to fire, but fame and glory were denied. The gun jammed.

More British machines were reported as gaining on the German as it flew down the Thames, on the way dropping two bombs on Cliffe, a village on the Hoo peninsula overlooking the Thames marshes. This lightened the load but, if it was a last-minute attempt on a useful target such as the cement works there, it missed.

By the time the quarry and the hunters were past Southend, the mist and cloud had intervened and the excitement was over.

The first Vickers FB5 in France was delivered to No. 2 Squadron of the RFC in February 1915. The Gunbus was better than anything the Germans had but there were only a few, fifty or sixty arrived during the whole year, so you could not say that the Entente exactly had air supremacy, even in the short few months before the Germans' secret weapon suddenly appeared. After that, for another short time, the Gunbus remained the best the Entente had, if not good enough.

Fighter ace Major Fred Powell of 5 Squadron, or, more accurately, his observer Air Mechanic Shaw, presumably co-opted for the ride, shot down and destroyed one German aircraft confirmed in the FB5 and one more driven down. He had six more victories unconfirmed before he moved on to the Royal Aircraft Factory FE8 (90mph single-seater) to finish with six definites and nine possibles. Big scores were not made in Farman-style pushers.

The Aviatik B1 was another 60mph general-purpose aircraft, not armed at first, used for reconnaissance until declared obsolete in early 1916.

Meanwhile, the RFC had got around to forming the first squadron officially designated for fighting, but No. 11 Squadron didn't arrive in France, at St Omer, until July 1915. It was not just the first fighter squadron; it was the first RFC squadron to be fully equipped from the start with aircraft all of one type, the FB5 Gunbus, which was still a fearsome opponent for those Germans flying the 60mph Albatros B1 and B2, the similarly slow Aviatik B1, Taube, LVG B1 and the later C models of Albatros and Aviatik.

It was an FB5 that carried Lieutenant Gilbert Insall to a Victoria Cross and a victory over an Aviatik biplane, probably a B2.

From *The London Gazette*, December 22 1915, this is Insall's citation:

> For most conspicuous bravery, skill and determination, on 7 November 1915, in France. He was patrolling in a Vickers Fighting Machine, with First Class Air Mechanic T. H. Donald as gunner, when a German machine was sighted, pursued, and attacked near Achiet.
>
> The German pilot led the Vickers machine over a rocket battery, but with great skill Lieutenant Insall dived and got to close range, when Donald fired a drum of cartridges into the German machine, stopping its engine. The German pilot then dived through a cloud, followed by Lieutenant Insall. Fire was again opened, and the German machine was brought down heavily in a ploughed field 4 miles south-east of Arras.

On seeing the Germans scramble out of their machine and prepare to fire, Lieutenant Insall dived to 500 feet, thus enabling Donald to open heavy fire on them. The Germans then fled, one helping the other, who was apparently wounded. Other Germans then commenced heavy fire, but in spite of this, Lieutenant Insall turned again, and an incendiary bomb was dropped on the German machine, which was last seen wreathed in smoke. Lieutenant Insall then headed west in order to get back over the German trenches, but as he was at only 2,000 feet altitude he dived across them for greater speed, Donald firing into the trenches as he passed over.

The German fire, however, damaged the petrol tank, and, with great coolness, Lieutenant Insall landed under cover of a wood 500 yards inside our lines. The Germans fired some 150 shells at our machine on the ground, but without causing material damage. Much damage had, however, been caused by rifle fire, but during the night it was repaired behind screened lights, and at dawn Lieutenant Insall flew his machine home with First Class Air Mechanic T. H. Donald as a passenger.

Donald was awarded the Distinguished Conduct Medal, the other-ranks equivalent of the DSO, some recognition of his own coolness while repairing, at night, under shell fire, the machine his pilot had flown much too close to the trenches and, we must assume, during the decidedly hairy take-off next morning.

Before he could tot up enough victims to be classed as an ace, Insall was shot down again, wounded, taken prisoner, escaped at the third attempt, and served as a Group Captain in the Second World War.

ANTON FOKKER AND HIS SINGLE DECKER

The basic problem with the pusher configurations so far, and with Louis Strange-style improvised overhead gunnery, was that you had one man with a free-standing gun, mounted on a constantly shifting base that was being controlled by another man, firing at an unpredictably shifting target. It was a fast-moving puzzle in double 3D.

A secondary design fault with pushers, especially the livelier ones like the DH2 (90mph single-seater), was that loose objects in the cockpits could fly up and out during violent turns and climbs, and smash back into the propeller. The loose object might be an ammunition drum or, and this really happened, shell cases while the gun was being fired. It didn't take much to destroy a wooden propeller.

What was needed were guns that could fire along the attacking line, in the sole control of the pilot of a fast, highly manoeuvrable aircraft.

The heaviness, recoil and lack of reliable automatic feeding of current machine guns, and the relative frailty of wings, meant that there was no option for wing-mounted twin guns with converging fire, as used on Second World War fighters. Some method had to be found of firing along the nose of the attacking machine where, obviously, the propeller was.

The Morane-Saulnier type L high-wing monoplane, not a usual configuration for the time and so, with its large, spreading wings shading all beneath, nicknamed Parasol, was not what you'd call fast and highly manoeuvrable. Even so, it became the first of the older tractor designs to be modified for air-to-air fighting and it did, through its shortcomings, show what was needed.

In early 1915, Aleksandr Aleksandrovich Kazakov (*q.v.*), an officer in the Imperial Russian Air Service, tried several experiments in his Parasol, dangling grappling hooks and explosives beneath him and trying, and failing, to bring down Germans that way.

A French officer, Roland Garros, pre-war music student and tennis player turned racing aviator, had the propeller of his Parasol fitted with metal plates. When he fired through his prop, the machine gun bullets that hit were deflected, while the others went on straight. The downside was that the deflector plates took about 30% efficiency off the propeller, reducing performance considerably.

He had three kills with this amazing method in April 1915 before himself being forced to land behind enemy lines at Ingelmunster.

The Times reported that he had been armed only with a rifle while his third victim, a Taube, had carried 'a quick-firing gun', which was the reverse of the case. The Thunderer made up in drama what it lacked in accuracy: 'These battles in the air, the manoeuvring of the hostile aeroplanes, the flash of their guns, and the little puffs of shrapnel smoke studding the clear blue sky formed a picture of extraordinary interest and fascination.'

Garros was taken prisoner. He escaped from POW camp

in February 1918, rejoined the air force as a fighter pilot and, on 2 October 1918, claimed two more victories, but only one was confirmed so with four in total he could not be listed as an ace. Three days later, flying a SPAD, he was shot down and killed, possibly by minor German ace Leutnant Hermann Habich (seven victories) in a Fokker D7, one of the very best German fighters of the war but too late arriving to reverse the nation's fortunes.

Garros had been captured before he could destroy his aircraft, and a story ran around that the deflector plates on his propeller somehow gave Anton Herman Gerard Fokker, the Dutch pioneer working for the Germans, the idea for his gun/propeller interrupter mechanism.

Fokker was a highly accomplished pilot, engineer

Roland Garros, intrepid French sportsman, motor racer and fighter pilot, somehow looks just as you might expect him to look.

The Fokker D7, a very fine flyer despite its boxy looks, was much favoured by a certain Oberleutnant Hermann Göring, who shot down the last four of his twenty-two victims in one.

and aircraft designer, who went to college in Germany in 1910 and set up his business there in 1912. By April 1915 he was about to introduce his secret weapon, his synchronisation gear to allow a machine gun to fire through the propeller arc without hitting the woodwork. If not a copy of the 1913 patented design by Swiss engineer Franz Schneider (which was never built) nor of the French 1914 patent by Raymond Saulnier (which was built but failed due to lack of a suitable gun), Fokker's device was, shall we say, closely based on them. Later, Schneider successfully sued Fokker, who refused to pay up.

Certainly, if Fokker did see Garros's propeller, he would have drawn the same conclusion as everyone else: it was not the answer. Nor was the Parasol for that matter – but the Fokker Eindecker filled the bill and the first would arrive in May 1915, to terrify Entente airmen. Until someone could get hold of Fokker's secret synchro-trigger, German air supremacy would be incontestable. The Gunbus, the BE2 and all the other types were no longer adequate, while the DH2 and FE8 were not there yet. For RFC aircrew there was nothing else.

Often called the Fokker Scourge (roughly from July 1915 to early 1916), the time produced two of the most famous German aces, Oswald Boelcke and Max Immelmann, many of whose kills were of uncompetitive machines. Von Richthofen later commented on the good fortune of Immelmann in coming across victims without machine guns. His squadron-mate Erwin Böhme would describe the job in more lyrical terms:

> For us, every fight is a personal fight, man against man, with the same weapons and the same chances. That is the splendid part of fighter aviation, that in this time of mass murder by machines, technology and chemistry, which modern warfare has become, individuals still conduct an honourably manly fight, eye to eye with the opponent. Every fight for us is a knightly joust... a sportsman-like duel.

That might have been true later in the war, when the Entente powers had much better fighters like the Nieuport 17 and the Sopwith Camel, but the Eindecker against the BE2 was rather more like shooting fish in a barrel than a knightly joust. The Germans called the BE2 *Kalten Fleisch*, cold meat. They might have called their task *Entenjagd* (duck shoot) too, because that's about what it was.

This is not to suggest that the Germans were being unsporting. The business of Entente aircraft, whether pure reconnaissance or artillery direction, was to help kill more German soldiers on the ground. Of course they had to be stopped. If the Entente, through lack of engineering inventiveness, chose to send their brave aircrew up in obsolete, inadequate machines, well, that was tough on the aircrew but nothing to do with Oswald and Max.

All things are relative, and the Eindecker was of its time and not an especially remarkable aircraft. It was based on a 1913 design, a mid-wing monoplane that could not reach 90mph in level flight until the third and fourth variants were built, and took half an hour to reach 10,000 feet. Still, it was faster than pretty well anything the Entente had, and could certainly out-turn them.

In just one year from its introduction on the Western Front, the Eindecker would meet the Sopwith Triplane, aka the Tripehound, which could get to 10,000 feet in ten minutes. In the meantime, it would meet the little Nieuport 11 biplane, *Le Bébé*, a much more agile dogfighter but, as a single-seater with its gun mounted on the top wing, reloading was difficult. The DH2, a one-seat pusher designed by Geoffrey de Havilland, was superior to the Fokker but it was a while arriving at the Front.

The Eindecker was Kaiser of the skies and in that year it was responsible for downing something like 1,000 aircraft, ten for every Eindecker in service at the end of 1915. It could have been more, but there were restrictions on its use. The Germans were near paranoid about the enemy finding the secret of the interrupter gear and so pilots were forbidden to fly beyond enemy lines. Initially used exclusively as an escort, it was only later that they flew in packs of four, detailed to attack areas where Entente aircraft were expected.

Inevitably, the tide would turn. The fish in the barrel would become, for example, the DFW CV two-seater reconnaissance machine, and the shooter would be the Royal Aircraft Factory SE5A, another de Havilland design, but in the meantime, RFC pilots called themselves Fokker fodder. The E-type's ability to shoot through its propeller arc, aimed by the pilot, brought calamity to the Entente air forces and turned reconnaissance and artillery spotting over enemy lines into suicide missions.

The Eindecker was closely based on the pre-war Fokker scout M5, which in turn was more or less copied from the Morane-Saulnier H, a civilian sports plane that could do over 70mph and was often seen at aero meetings where records could be set and broken.

VISCOUNT CHERWELL AND HIS SPIN DOCTOR

Anyone who has flown in a light aircraft, ancient or modern, will know that the difference between that and a seat on a jumbo jet is like the difference between riding a bicycle on a farm track on a windy day and being conveyed to St Pancras in the first-class dining car.

While it is true that all aircraft are free to rock in three dimensions, in a light aircraft the experience is somewhat amplified. In flight there is pitch, nose/tail up/down, and yaw, nose/tail left/right, and roll, rotation about the nose/tail axis. Control of these motions, and deliberate use thereof, is by means of movable parts of the flying surfaces. Elevators, that is, flaps on the tailplane or, in Wright mode, out front, produce pitch. A flap on the tailfin, the rudder, produces yaw, and ailerons, flaps on the wings' trailing edges, produce roll.

Many early and widely deployed aircraft did not have ailerons but, as we have seen, rolled by wires attached to the wings' trailing edges. The pilot pulled on the wires to alter the shape of his mainplanes.

All of this, of course, was at about 50mph. By the time we got to the fully aileroned Royal Aircraft Factory BE2E in mid-1916, we were going at 90mph with a 90hp engine. In early 1917, the Reconnaisance Experimental 8, RE8, Harry Tate, was introduced, a ton-up machine with a 140hp engine, but still we cannot say that aircraft were being designed with complete understanding of the forces at work in flight. For example, early models of the RE8 had shown a strong tendency to spin, which caused many crashes with inexperienced pilots who got themselves in a muddle. In those early times, once you were in a spin, nobody really knew how you might get out of it.

Frederick Alexander Lindemann, later the first Viscount Cherwell (1886–1957), physicist and politician, was born at Baden-Baden, where his mother, American/ British Olga Noble, the remarried widow of a rich US banker, was taking the cure. Frederick resented all his life the accident of his birthplace being in Germany. His father was Adolphus Frederick Lindemann (1846–1927), who had emigrated to Britain in his twenties and later became naturalised.

There was plenty of money in the family. Olga and Adolphus brought in about £20,000 a year, equivalent to £20 million today. He was a distinguished scientist and astronomer, working from his own private lab and observatory near Sidmouth, and did not stint his children regarding allowances. Son Frederick studied physics in Germany and became a tennis player of note, which is what he was doing there as war threatened.

Returning swiftly to Sidmouth, his eyesight proved too poor for the army to award him a commission, so he joined the Royal Aircraft Factory at Farnborough to work on the newborn subject of aeronautics, where he became interested in the phenomenon of spin.

There were no mathematical formulae or aeronautical principles to define why an aircraft might go into a spin. They knew very well that a spin was near-impossible to get out of, and they knew from experience what circumstances might conspire to produce a spin, but if there was to be a universally applicable solution, the physics of the problem had to be understood.

A pilot finding himself in an unintentional stall might see, let's say, the port wing drop. His instinctive reaction would be to pull back on the stick to correct this but, inexplicably, this would have the opposite effect to the one intended. The starboard wing would rise, the port wing would dip further, the aircraft would roll, the nose would dip, and suddenly the pilot was spinning towards the ground with no options left. Something similar could happen in a tight turn.

Lindemann saw that two characteristics of flight had to occur together to produce spin: yaw, and roll. It couldn't happen if the machine was flying straight and level, nor with simple up-and-down pitch, a dive or a climb, but Entente pilots pursued by Immelmann, Boelcke and Co tended not to fly in straight lines. Lindemann had heard of at least two occasions when pilots had somehow escaped from a spin, although he didn't know how they did it and neither, probably, did they, but he felt sure that the answer was in the tailfin. The rudder would have to be held fully against the spin until it stopped, and only then could you pull back on the stick. Some of his calculations indicated that full rudder might prove too much for the wings in a spin, so he didn't test his theory in a Taube.

Due to the natural unwillingness of ordinary pilots to conduct anti-spin experiments on the word of some boffin with a German accent, Lindemann realised he would have to learn to fly. He managed to sidestep the eye test and get his licence but he never did learn to fly very well. Still, he was good enough to put the machine in a spin on purpose.

On a summer's day in 1917, Lindemann took off from Farnborough in a BE2C and climbed as high as he could go, 10,000 feet or so, which took him three-quarters of an hour. Levelling off, he slowed the engine right down, losing airspeed so that a stall was inevitable when he pulled the stick back. A bit of left aileron gave him the drag he needed and almost immediately he was spinning, anticlockwise.

The crowd of fellow scientists and workers below watched in great anxiety as the machine plummeted earthwards. If it had taken him 45 minutes to get up there, it was going to be more like 45 seconds to come down. In the cockpit, Lindemann's foot pressed as hard as he might on full right rudder, but no results could be observed by him or the spectators until, after far too long for everyone's nerves, the spin slowed and eventually stopped.

Lindemann was now in a straight nosedive. Engine revs up, stick slowly back, and he was flying again. Just to show there was no mystery to it, he did another long climb and spun the machine the other way, with the same gratifying result. Now, not only could pilots be trained to get out of a spin, they could be trained to get into and out of one, which for a while proved a useful surprise escape tactic when being attacked by German fighters.

As Lord Cherwell, Lindemann became Churchill's scientific adviser in the Second World War, when his trenchant and sometimes outdated views did not always lead to the best advice. For example, he was quite sure that infra-red rays would be a better option than radar, and that the V2 rocket-bomb was an impossibility. Nevertheless, he did much sterling work and, through his own courage, saved the lives of many pilots.

Although the BE2C was a much improved version of the original BE2, with ailerons instead of wing-warping, it was still a pre-war designed machine, underpowered for its size and fragile as all such aircraft were.

PART THREE
Aces High

A typical RFC aerodrome in France, this one was near Amiens, photo taken in the winter of 1916/17.

The generally accepted definition of an Ace was a pilot with five victories, and if that's all there was to it we can count about 1,860 pilots of all sides in the Great War who achieved that status, of whom some 420 were killed in action during that war. The problem comes with what to term a victory; the definition varied from side to side and time to time, but generally required confirmation from witnesses. Very early in the war, when aeroplanes and everything connected therewith could be classed as novelty, any encounter between flying enemies was hot news and there was much confusion over what could be counted as a win. Simply forcing the other pilot to flee and land behind his own lines was considered a victory in those early days.

The Germans were strict throughout the war, in that a victory could not be credited to a pilot unless it was achieved by that pilot alone, and/or his observer if flying a two-seater, and the enemy machine was confirmed as destroyed or captured. An early, further essential was that enemy aircraft had to fall behind German lines, but that was not the case later.

The French applied those same criteria for most of the war, except they allowed victories shared between several pilots to be fully credited to each, and in 1914/15 the definition of victory was rather more loose.

The British were the least strict of all, at first allowing Forced to Land and Driven Down, then introducing Out of Control instead of those categories, as well as fully crediting each pilot in a shared win.

Using the German definition, French ace René Fonck would have his score cut from 75 to 50. Canadian William Bishop would have his total of 72 almost halved, and top British ace Edward Mannock (q.v.) would go down from 61 to something like 25. It is beyond the scope of this little book to turn that figure of 1,865 aces into a new number according to German rules. Of the main contributors to the totals, German records classify 393 of their own pilots as aces plus 49 from the Austro-Hungarian Empire. On the other side, the French had 180, Canada 193, Australia 75, America 112, Great Britain and Ireland 722.

The conventional top ten table is thus:

Manfred von Richthofen	Germany	80
René Fonck	France	75
William Bishop	Canada	72
Ernst Udet	Germany	62
Edward Mannock	Great Britain	61
Raymond Collishaw	Canada	60
James McCudden	Great Britain	57
Andrew Beauchamp-Proctor	South Africa	54
Erich Löwenhardt	Germany	54
Donald MacLaren	Canada	54

However, if we create a new category of super-aces scoring forty or more, and apply the strict German rules, only one Entente airman would get in the top ten, thus:

Manfred von Richthofen	80
Ernst Udet	62
Erich Löwenhardt	54
René Fonck	50
Josef Jacobs	48
Werner Voss	48
Fritz Rumey	45
Rudolf Berthold	44
Bruno Loerzer	44
Paul Bäumer	43

The only other forty-scorers are given as Oswald Boelcke, Franz Büchner, and Manfred's brother Lothar Ritter von Richthofen, although Lothar had thirty-nine at the most (see Albert Ball, page 171).

In this section we shall not always be concentrating on the most famous and well documented figures. The histories of certain of those men demand to be included, but we shall also seek out some of the lesser lights whose stories nevertheless make more interesting reading than a scoresheet.

MAX IMMELMANN AND HIS TURN

Oberleutnant Immelmann was by no means one of the highest scorers of the First World War, but he was one of the first to gain a reputation. After an undistinguished early flying career, when he operated as a message courier and was forced down by a French Farman, he was introduced to the Eindecker. Through his appreciation of the new combat possibilities given to him by the gun firing forward through the prop, he became well known to the RFC during the autumn of 1915, variously nicknamed The Professor and The Eagle of Lille.

Max has also been credited with the invention of two aerobatic manoeuvres, both called the Immelmann Turn, although it is unlikely he was responsible for either. The more modern fighter pilot's version, used in the Second World War to escape attack from behind or to regain the initiative should one find oneself under such attack, is an instant half loop followed by a half roll, putting the attacked on the attacker's tail instead. It was also used by at least one bomber pilot in the Second World War, Wing Commander Balme DSO, DFC and Bar of 227 Squadron, who executed it in his Lancaster to get out of searchlight cones.

The original 1915 version was a way of having another go after a failed diving attack, or of gaining a means of escape. The attacker pulled out of his dive, climbed to a position above his victim, and slowed almost to stalling speed. Now came the difficult part. Full rudder allowed the most skilful pilots to whip the aircraft round through 180 degrees, ready to dive on the target again or to make off.

Both sides used the Turn, Biggles himself deployed it in his Sopwith Camel (see Preface), but it was dangerous and could allow the enemy in a dogfight a good shot while the turner was almost stationary at the top of the climb.

Immelmann understood the benefits of studying where RFC craft were likely to be and made sure he hung around in such places, like a bird of prey that knows the best sources of food as, indeed, an Eagle would. If some of his intended victims managed to escape, their accounts of the fights later in the mess only added to his fame.

For example, the crews of two Moranes of 3 Squadron, on separate occasions described a Fokker turning up out of nowhere, shooting them all about, wounding one or both crew members and forcing them to run for it and crash-land on the home aerodrome. They, at least, had not been entirely defeated by Professor Immelmann, even if they would have been counted as victories, had they been German and Immelmann British.

Max had his eighth confirmed victory on 12 January 1916, a Vickers Gunbus, which made him equal to Boelcke (see page 136), for two days anyway, and, together with his friendly rival, he was awarded the Blue Max, the *Orden Pour le Mérite*, the German approximate equivalent of the

Victoria Cross, established by Frederick the Great of Prussia in 1740. These two were the first flyers to be so decorated.

Although officially awarded for exceptional bravery in combat, the Blue Max was not given to airmen for individual acts of heroism but rather for the quantity of enemies defeated, and the number required increased as the war went on. Von Richthofen needed sixteen before he got his, which was rather unfair as the job was becoming more and more difficult by then.

Six of Immelmann's seventeen victories were over the BE2C, and another five were similarly unarmed types. Only six of the craft he shot down were purpose-fitted with machine guns, of which three were the lumbering Vickers Gunbus, although he did also get three of the superior, Rolls-Royce-powered FE2B, and two Bristol Scouts of the C type fitted with a side-mounted gun. His first knockdown, a BE2C on 1 August 1915, was probably the third Eindecker victory of all, after Kurt Wintgens had confirmed July victories over two Morane Parasols.

Immelmann met his end on 18 June 1916, thus gaining another first; he was the first German ace to be killed in action. In his Mark 3 Eindecker, he was in an evening battle and some reports had him shot down by an RFC FE2B, which was the version the British promoted, naturally. Most of the flyers on the German side didn't want to think that Immelmann could have been beaten, and so believed another story, that his interrupter gear had failed and he'd shot off his own propeller.

Antony Fokker himself examined the wreckage. His new design, a biplane successor to the Eindecker, was being tested at the time by Boelcke and looked like becoming big business for the aircraft company. Fokker concluded that Immelmann had been hit by his own side's anti-aircraft fire.

Initially, *The Times* reported: 'Two of our fighting aeroplanes encountered two Fokkers in the vicinity of Lens. One of the hostile machines was driven down damaged. The other was shot down and crashed to earth from 4,000 feet.'

Later, they had the full story: 'Immelmann's death has created a profound sensation in Germany. His method was to rise to a great height, then descend diagonally, and annihilate the enemy.'

The Kaiser had been writing to him to congratulate him on his twelfth victory, when his thirteenth was announced. Altering the figure to thirteen, the Kaiser said 'One cannot even write as quickly as Immelmann fires'. This story could well be true, as these two victims fell on consecutive days.

German eyewitnesses quoted in the *New York Times* describe Immelmann fighting with two enemy machines, large biplanes, and shooting at one while being shot at by the other, and variously noting a wing and a tail falling from the Fokker.

Much the most likely story makes the marksman Corporal James H Waller, later to die from the effects of poison gas, observer in an FE2B of 25 Squadron. He is given as 'Corporal W' in a newspaper report a few weeks later, with his pilot as 'Lieutenant McC', which may have given rise to the story that it was British ace James McCudden who defeated the legendary Max. McCudden was still in training in the UK at the time.

The pilot was Second Lieutenant George Reynolds McCubbin, only in France a few weeks, who was indeed awarded the DSO, gazetted 16 July 1916, with his citation mentioning his observer shooting down a Fokker on two separate occasions, on the second of which McCubbin was badly wounded while attacking the German who had been 'following one of our machines'. Acting Sergeant J H Waller was awarded the Distinguished Conduct Medal on, 27 July 1916, 'for conspicuous gallantry and skill' in shooting down two Fokkers, both of which were 'seen to crash to the ground'.

That day, 18 June 1916, had already had a fight between Immelmann and 25 Squadron and it was one up to Max as he felled the FE2B flown by Lieutenant Clarence Rogers to record his sixteenth victory. In the evening, he shot down the FE2B of Lieutenant R B Savage, not killing the crew this time, but providing a target in front of George McCubbin as he turned his aircraft to follow the

German. James Waller was immediately up and on the forward-firing gun and got in a long burst before Immelmann could react himself, and that was that.

The Royal Aircraft Factory FE2 series of pusher fighters were initially armed with a forward-firing gun but more armoury was added to counter the Fokker Scourge. FE2 crews found themselves to be more than an adequate match for the Eindecker although Immelmann had three in his total, plus three Vickers Gunbus.

FIRSTS OF ALL NATIONS

A 353   Fliegerleutnant Immelmann.

Max Immelmann with some of his many medals poses in the studio before he had his Blue Max to wear at his neck.

The first Russian ace to be killed in action was actually a Latvian who had scored most of his victories with *l'Aéronautique Militaire.* Eduard Martynovich Pulpe went to Moscow University, qualified as a teacher and moved to France to broaden his outlook. He learned to fly there and volunteered as soon as war broke out. His first two scores were in the Morane Parasol, so unless he was using Roland Garros's deflector plates – most unlikely in late 1915 – they would have been down to his observer. In any case, they were on the same day.

The escadrille re-equipped with Nieuport machines and Pulpe won his next two victories in a Nieuport 11, the Bébé, with its gun on top of its wing above the pilot's head. After transfer to the Imperial Russian Air Service, Pulpe was posted to the Eastern Front where he scored another victory in a similar machine to win his ace status. A few weeks later he was flying the line between the Imperial Russian and Austro-Hungarian armies, at this point the Styr river in south-east Ukraine, when he had the misfortune to meet a flight of Albatros C3 two-seaters that included one flown by Erwin Böhme. Pulpe's was the faster machine, a Nieuport 12 with at least 10mph over the Albatros, and a purpose-designed fighter; but there were three of them.

A long dogfight ensued, which some witnesses said lasted an hour, and Pulpe took a lot of punishment before Böhme's observer administered the *coup de grâce*, at least, we must assume he got in the last blow because Pulpe is given as the first of Böhme's 24 victories and, as we have seen, the German air force was precise about such matters.

This was 2 August 1916, almost a year since the first ace of all, *le roi du ciel* Alphonse Pégoud, became the first French ace to be killed in action, and six weeks after Immelmann.

The first British ace so to die could, like Pulpe, be credited to more than one nation, his family having emigrated to Canada when he was a boy, but he was born in London and so is counted.

Second Lieutenant Henry Cope Evans DSO, of 24 Squadron, had a short flying career, reaching ace-hood in two months but not living to see his DSO citation in the *Gazette*: 'For conspicuous gallantry and skill on many occasions in attacking hostile aircraft, frequently against large odds. In one fortnight he brought down 4 enemy machines, returning on one occasion with his machine badly damaged.'

No. 24 Squadron, at this time commanded by Major Lanoe George Hawker *(q.v.)*, was flying the Airco DH2, faster and more manoeuvrable than the Fokker Eindecker, the Scourge of which it had been very important in ending. Being a pusher, it had a forward firing gun but the pilots had to aim it and even change its mounting while flying the aircraft. Under Hawker, they soon learned that it was better to fix the gun and aim the aircraft, as per Eindecker, and the 24 Squadron mechanics devised a piece of kit which enabled that tactic.

Henry Evans did not fall in aerial combat but was shot down by anti-aircraft fire, his machine completely destroyed and his body never found.

Evans, the first ace from mainland Britain to be KIA was an old man of thirty-seven. Sidney Edward Cowan was born in Downpatrick, County Down on 23 August 1897, which makes him still only eighteen years old when he had his fifth victory on the 9th of that month in 1916, being wounded in that action. His first had come way back in May and it earned him the Military Cross. *London Gazette*: 'For conspicuous gallantry and skill. He dived on to an enemy machine in the enemy's lines and drove it to the ground, where it was smashed, and then circled round and fired at the pilot and observer as they ran for shelter. Although forced to land through his engine stopping he contrived to restart it and got back under heavy fire.'

A Bar to his MC was awarded after his fourth victory on 3 August, and he lived to see the citation in the *Gazette*: 'For conspicuous gallantry and skill. He has done fine work in aerial combats, and has shot down four enemy machines.'

He would have seen the notice of his second Bar too, in the *Gazette* on 14 November, by which time he'd had his nineteenth birthday and was Captain Cowan, posted as a flight commander to 29 Squadron: 'For conspicuous gallantry in action. He fought a long contest with seven enemy machines, finally bringing one down in flames. He has displayed great skill and gallantry throughout.'

This happened on 16 September. His next and seventh victory was his last, on 17 November, when he brought down a Halberstadt D2, the first biplane fighter the Germans had. Moments later, a junior pilot, Second Lieutenant William Spencer Fitz-Robert Saundby, flew into Cowan's machine and they both fell to their deaths, although Saundby's body was never found.

Of a family delighting in forenames, eighteen-year-old Saundby was the younger brother of Robert Henry Magnus Spencer Saundby, ace fighter pilot with five victories, who had flown with 24 Squadron. Posted home as a test pilot, Saundby senior took the very rare prize of a Zeppelin airship, shot down at night. In the Second World War, Air Marshal Sir Robert Saundby KCB, KBE, MC, DFC, AFC, was Sir Arthur Harris's number two at Bomber Command.

ROSENCRANTZ AND FAHLBUSCH ARE DEAD

By the late summer of 1916, the Fokker Scourge was deemed to be over although Germans aces such as Wintgens and Boelcke were still flying the Eindecker Mark 3. Partly responsible for that change in the balance of air power had been the Sopwith Strutter, the first Entente aircraft with guns firing forward through the prop, although not entirely reliably. The observer had a machine gun too; with a top speed of 100mph, it was a formidable machine.

Similarly armed, slightly faster but looking completely different was the LFG Roland C2, known as the whale

(*Walfisch*). It had a tubby fuselage of novel plywood construction that filled all the space between the two wings, so the pilot and observer sat on top, above it all. This was excellent for sighting bandits twelve o'clock high, but not so good for spotting Albert Ball (*q.v.*) coming at you from below. Although he did say it was the best German aircraft at the time.

The first pilot to reach ace status in a whale was Leutnant Wilhelm Fahlbusch who, in one photograph, looks a little like Ardal O'Hanlon in *Father Ted*. He was twenty-four years old while totting up his five victories, all of which are also credited to his observer, Leutnant Hans Rosencrantz, probably because the early examples of the whale did not have the forward-firing gun fitted and so Hans did all the shooting.

Their fifth, ace-making victory was an elephant, a Martynside G100 so-called unsurprisingly because of its large size. Originally supposed to be a long-range fighter,

it was not agile enough for that but proved a good platform for bombing and photography. Captain Alfred Skinner of 27 Squadron was flying the elephant that day, 31 August, but he was the last man killed by Rosencrantz and Fahlbusch because a few days later, on 6 September,

Hans Rosencrantz (left) and Wilhelm Fahlbusch pose, not with a whale but with an Albatros.

they ran into a flight of Strutters of 70 Squadron RFC over Élincourt, between Abbeville and the coast.

Lieutenant Bernard Beanlands was in one, Captain William Sanday MC was in another, and Lieutenant Selby was in a third; between them they sent the whale down in flames. It was Beanlands's first of nine, Sanday's fourth of five, which brought him the DSO on top of his MC. All three pilots lived through the war.

OSWALD BOELCKE AND HIS *DICTA*

Boelcke was in the war almost from the first day, flying two-seater reconnaissance aircraft with his brother Wilhelm as observer. Oswald transferred to *Fliegerabteilung* 62 in April 1915, which was flying the LVG C2, a steady-as-she-goes two-seater reconnaissance aircraft. His life was changed utterly when three of the new Fokker Eindecker arrived on squadron and he was given access to them, along with Immelmann, Kurt Wintgens (nineteen victories, two on 24 September 1916, killed in action next day) and Otto Parschau (eight victories, tutor to Boelcke/Immelmann, died from wounds after dogfight 21 July 1916).

Boelcke's first victory, however, was not in the Fokker. His observer in his LVG, Leutnant von Wülisch, shot down a Morane Parasol on 4 July but Boelcke also had the credit, being the pilot. Boelcke in the Eindecker claimed his first confirmed solo win over a Bristol Scout, unarmed version, on 19 August.

With more victories, Boelcke began evolving his theory of air combat, leading to command of his own unit in which to practise, *Jagdstaffel* (Jasta) 2, which became *Jagdstaffel* Boelcke after his death. All other German airmen regarded him as infallible, and his word as gospel. His famous *Dicta* may well owe something to Immelmann's thoughts too, but they defined fighter-piloting for everyone who came after. They were written down in 1916:

> Secure an advantage before attacking, such as gaining height so as to surprise the enemy from above, and placing yourself between the sun and the enemy.
> Once you decide to attack, do not hesitate to carry it out, but do not fire until you are within range and you have the enemy in your sights.
> Preferably attack when the enemy is occupied with his duties.
> Never run away. If you are attacked from behind, turn and face your enemy.
> Watch your enemy and look always for tricks and deceit.
> Remember your own escape route.

Hauptmann Boelcke was the second pilot of all to win the accolade of fighter ace but the first to double figures, just ahead of his competitive colleague Immelmann. Both were fortunate in their early careers, in the autumn of 1915, that they did have the first really effective, purpose-made fighter aircraft and their enemies didn't have anything like it.

By the time Boelcke reached his total of forty victories, the odds had evened out a little, but his instructions, known as Boelcke's *Dicta* by both sides in the war, remained the doctrine for success in aerial combat for as long as fighter aircraft were entirely under the control of their pilots.

He also became interested in the possibilities of fighters hunting in groups. He added another stricture to his *Dicta*, recommending attack in groups of four or six but being careful not to have multiple attackers chasing single opponents. The wisdom of this instruction he was to prove, fatally.

Like all the other Eindecker pilots, Boelcke didn't really come up against serious opposition until the summer of 1916. His seventeenth, eighteenth and nineenth victims were Nieuport fighters, the Bébé with forward firing gun above the pilot's head, but before that all his victories were over machines that couldn't really fight back.

When the DH2, the FE2B and the Sopwith 1½ Strutter came in, the air supremacy of the Fokker E was challenged and overturned, but Boelcke proved himself still the master, flying the Albatros D2 'straight-winged machine' from mid-September 1916. He reached his forty with two BE2C on consecutive days.

That he fell due to a mid-air collision cannot surely be doubted, witnessed as it was by von Richthofen and the grey eminence Erwin Böhme, the latter being personally involved. It was Boelcke's sixth operation of the day, on 28 October 1916. Böhme:

> On Saturday afternoon we sat around in readiness,
> in our little cottage at the airfield. I'd just started
> a chess game with Boelcke when we were called

out to help in an infantry attack on the front, shortly after 16.00. Boelcke led us, as usual. We soon came to attack several British aeroplanes over Flers, fast single-seaters who defended themselves ably. There followed a wild fight that allowed us only brief shots... Boelcke and I had an Englishman between us when another, chased by friend Richthofen, cut in front of us.

The Englishmen were Canadians, in DH2 aircraft of 29 Squadron, and several was two, against six. Between Boelcke and Böhme was Arthur Gerald Knight DSO, MC, with six victories at that time, and being chased by 'friend Richthofen' was Alfred Edwin McKay, who had two victories. Knight got to eight before the Baron shot him down on 20 December 1916, making him the first Canadian ace to be KIA, while McKay reached ten before he was killed a year later.

In the confusion of the moment, with multiple attackers chasing single opponents, Boelcke and Böhme collided. It wasn't much, just a touch, but it was enough to send Boelcke spinning to earth and death. Even the crash wasn't a total wreck, and Böhme wrote that with a helmet, never worn, or harness, never fastened, the great man might have survived.

Or is this version of events all propaganda? The Germans were keen to point out that their highest scorer had died undefeated. Neither Knight nor McKay made any claims, but an anonymous Australian anti-aircraft gunner has said that his battery shot Boelcke down. Here is von Richthofen's version of events:

One day we were flying, once more guided by Boelcke against the enemy. We always had a wonderful feeling of security when he was with us. After all, he was the one and only. The weather was very gusty and there were many clouds. There were no aeroplanes about except fighting ones.

From a long distance we saw two impertinent Englishmen in the air who actually seemed to enjoy the terrible weather. We were six and they were two. If they had been twenty and if Boelcke had given us the signal to attack we should not have been at all surprised.

The struggle began in the usual way. Boelcke tackled the one and I the other. I had to let go because one of the German machines got in my way. I looked around and noticed Boelcke settling his victim about two hundred yards away from me. It was the usual thing. Boelcke would shoot down his opponent and I had to look on. Close to Boelcke flew a good friend of his. It was an interesting struggle. Both men were shooting. It was probable that the Englishman would fall at any moment. Suddenly I noticed an unnatural movement of the two German flying machines. The two machines merely touched one another. However, if two machines go at the tremendous pace of flying machines, the slightest contact has the effect of a violent concussion.

Boelcke drew away from his victim and descended in large curves. He did not seem to be falling, but when I saw him descending below me I noticed that part of his wings had broken off. I could not see what happened afterward, but in the clouds he lost an entire wing. Now his machine was no longer steerable.

When we reached home we found the report 'Boelcke is dead!' had already arrived. We could scarcely realise it.

In the German press, Boelcke was remembered as 'a brilliant meteor, which has described its path and is suddenly extinguished', and 'one whose name will be inscribed in golden letters in the book of heroes', who 'died unvanquished'. If there had been the slightest possibility of the Entente saying they had shot Boelcke down, they would surely have made rather a fuss about it.

Oswald Boelcke poses for the camera with his Blue Max.

A few days after Boelcke's demise, Lord Montagu of Beaulieu wrote a piece in *The Times*, comparing the early days of the war with the current position:

...our machines were too slow, and the result was that valuable lives were often lost in the work of reconnaissance and photography, as well as in fighting and bombing expeditions... our pilots did much more work than the German pilots, and our air work was done for the Army and seldom failed it. There was no sensational flying and no 'starring' by pilots like Immelmann. The work of our pilots was at a high level of excellence all through, and our losses were therefore bound to be heavier.

Now, however, it is not too much to say that the enemy's air has become our air. His aeroplanes cannot live with ours at present. How long this will continue is doubtful.

LANOE GEORGE HAWKER ATTACKS EVERYTHING

The first to ace status among British pilots was an inventive Hampshire man, Lanoe George Hawker, who learned to fly privately and managed a transfer from the Royal Engineers to the RFC just in time for the war. With 6 Squadron in France, as a contemporary and mess mate of Louis Strange (*q.v.*), he flew reconnaissance missions like almost everyone else, at first in pre-war Farman kites, later in the BE2C, and it was in one of these that he made his first mark and won the DSO. *London Gazette*, 8 May 1915:

For conspicuous gallantry on 19th April 1915, when he succeeded in dropping bombs on the German airship shed at Gontrode from a height of only 200 feet, under circumstances of the greatest risk.

Lieutenant Hawker displayed remarkable ingenuity in utilizing an occupied German captive balloon to shield him from fire whilst manoeuvring to drop the bombs.

We can surmise that Hawker was using Louis Strange's bomb-dropping device, which had already had field trials at Courtrai railway station, and doubtless there were long conversations in the mess about how they might get over the frustrations of trying to shoot down Germans with a rifle. They had some impetus given to their schemes with the arrival on squadron of a few Bristol Scout machines, the fighter with no gun.

There were several experiments by both men with machine gun mountings; perhaps the oddest, and most surprisingly successful, was Hawker's side-mounted Lewis. He and a mechanic called Ernest Elton, later an ace himself with an astonishing sixteen victories in thirty-one days as a sergeant pilot, devised a fitment to the port side of the fuselage of a Bristol Scout, firing at a wide enough angle – 45 degrees to the aircraft's flight path – to miss the propeller.

The Eindecker was already at the Front although in very small numbers, but Hawker must have known about its mysterious ability to fire through the prop. His own device could not compare in efficiency, and in use against two-seaters it would expose him to the greatest danger. He would have to come in from the starboard quarter, where the enemy observer with his machine gun would have the very best angle to shoot him. Nevertheless, he flew solo with his new gun on 21

June 1915, came across a DFW and forced it down out of control. Four days later he met three Albatros C and the results earned him the Victoria Cross, the first instance of this medal being awarded for aerial combat. *London Gazette*, 24 August 1915:

> For most conspicuous bravery and very great ability on 25th July 1915. When flying alone he attacked three German aeroplanes in succession. The first managed eventually to escape, the second was driven to the ground damaged, and the third, which he attacked at a height of about 10,000 feet, was driven to earth in our lines, the pilot and observer being killed.
>
> The personal bravery shown by this Officer was of the very highest order, as the enemy's aircraft were armed with machine guns, and all carried a passenger as well as a pilot.

By August, Hawker's own aircraft was carrying a 'passenger' too, as 6 Squadron took delivery of the FE2B pusher. Second and third victories were over Albatros C machines, one forced to land and one captured, flying a Bristol Scout, but the next three were down to the FE2B observer, including an Aviatik destroyed and, most pleasing of all, one Eindecker destroyed, both on the same day, 11 August.

After one more destroyed in a Bristol Scout, Hawker was brought home and given the job of forming a new squadron, No. 24, the first to be entirely equipped with a single-seat fighter. The machine was the DH2, 90mph-plus, a fast climber, tight turner and aerobatically excellent. Like all such developments, the furious technological pace of war allowed it only a short period of supremacy, but for the moment it was the best.

Major Hawker took his squadron to France in February 1916 and issued his famous order: 'Attack everything'. They did, scoring many victories for relatively few losses. As commanding officer he didn't fly very often and so missed his best opportunities of adding to his score, because later in the year the Germans introduced the Albatros D2, 110mph with twin Spandau machine guns firing through the prop, and the good times of the DH2 were over.

His last flight was on 23 November, when he had the great misfortune to meet a D2 at 9,000 feet, flown by the new star of the Front, Manfred von Richthofen, who wrote to his mother describing the event:

> My eleventh Englishman is Major Hawker, twenty-six years old and a commander of a British squadron. Prisoners have said that he is 'the British Boelcke'. I had the most difficult fight with him that I have ever had up to now. After a long curving fight of three to five minutes, I forced my adversary down to 500 metres. Now he tried to escape, flying towards the Front. I pursued and brought him down after firing 900 rounds.

Major Lanoe George Hawker VC, DSO was actually a few weeks short of his twenty-sixth birthday. He fell behind enemy lines, killed by a single bullet in the head. The

Germans buried him where he fell, so, without a known grave, his name appears on the Arras Memorial.

JAMES MCCUDDEN, WORKING-CLASS SUPERMAN

A Morane Parasol of No. 3 Squadron took off from Auchel for a long recco flight to Valenciennes on 15 December 1915. The crew, Second Lieutenant Charles Edward Tudor-Jones, observer, and pilot Second Lieutenant Alan Victor Hobbs, aged twenty-one, knew full well that the Fokker Eindecker was causing havoc way beyond its relatively small numbers. The flyers' mission was to count the rolling stock at the railway station; this intelligence would help staff officers locate a German army that seemed to have disappeared.

Aircraft and crew failed to return. Next day, German wireless announced Leutnant Immelmann's seventh kill, a British monoplane over Valenciennes.

Immelmann's seventh. The wrecked Parasol of Tudor-Jones and Hobbs shows how little hope there was of crash survival for aircrew without parachutes.

Major Ludlow-Hewitt, later Air Chief Marshal Sir Edgar Ludlow-Hewitt GCB, GBE, CMG, DSO, MC, chief of Bomber Command in 1940 but now officer commanding No. 3 Squadron, announced a new tactic. This railway information was still required by HQ so they would go in force to get it. Captain Harvey-Kelly would lead with Lieutenant Portal as observer (later Chief of the Air Staff, Marshal of the Royal Air Force Charles Frederick Algernon Portal, 1st Viscount Portal of Hungerford, KG, GCB, OM, DSO and Bar, MC). Lieutenant Mealing would fly with Lieutenant Cleaver, and Lieutenant Saunders with Sergeant McCudden. Saunders would later transfer to No. 1 Squadron and, as Captain R A Saunders MC, be killed in March 1916 at the age of twenty-one. His observer was the future British super-ace James 'Mac' McCudden, fifty-seven victories.

Immelmann was flying the line between Lille and Lens. He seemed always to be there, waiting, high in the sky, ready to pounce. To combat him specifically, Ludlow-Hewitt had ordered the three crews to fly in formation, the first time they'd done such a thing.

The weather was poor and they had to wait for three days before they could go, on the clear, frosty morning of 19 December. They crossed the lines over the Bois du Biez at 7,500 feet and, a few miles east of there, after sailing through some fairly accurate archie, they saw the hawk, a black dot far above them.

It dived on the middle of the three Moranes and got in some good shots but Lieutenant Mealing turned and avoided the worst. Now the Fokker, for that's what it was, turned too and came at the third aircraft, nose to nose, firing through its propeller. McCudden had to stand up with his Lewis gun to his shoulder, to fire over his prop and carry on firing as the Fokker flew up, past and away.

It reappeared, climbing up under their tail, but McCudden saw it. Saunders veered as the observer fired, as he said, 'half a drum of Lewis'. The Fokker turned off, climbed to 300 feet above the intended prey, and began another dive. McCudden was expecting him and fired a long burst; the German pulled out immediately. He held off again, 500 feet distant, where he stayed while the three RFC crews flew over Valenciennes and gathered the information they wanted. Immelmann (they were sure it was The Professor) did a few aerobatics at a safe distance, then glided down to his home base at Douai, presumably out of petrol.

There was no doubt in anyone's mind that the Fokker had been Immelmann's, and this changed their views, previously and universally held, that if Immelmann came across you, you were a dead duck. We might wonder why they didn't think it was Boelcke, who had six victories by this point and was also well known in the small aerial world of the Western Front.

That same afternoon, McCudden was up again, sketching German trenches with the CO, Major Ludlow-Hewitt, when a Fokker dived on them. Once more Mac fired from the shoulder and put the German off. There was a bit of a flying display as Immelmann, sitting high in his seat and dressed in black, tried to get on the Parasol's tail, but he couldn't manage it and flew away. McCudden: 'All I can say is that to my mind he (Immelmann) would not fight when the odds were even.'

Life went on into the new year, flying every day that the weather allowed, and on 19 January McCudden was observing with Lieutenant Harold Johnson on a reconnaissance, when he was surprised to see a German two-seater biplane coming up fast behind; surprised because, apart from the Fokker, the Morane was thought to be as fast as anything the Germans had. Possibly the machine was one of the new LVG C2 or C3, with a much more powerful engine than its predecessor.

McCudden tried a few long-range shots with his rifle and got ready with his Lewis when the German got within 200 yards. Firing, the machine gun jammed after two rounds, so he swapped back to the rifle. The German flew alongside then turned away, as he did so giving his observer a good shot with a machine gun that didn't jam. Holes appeared in the Morane's wings while McCudden used up his ammunition to no avail. Twice more the German came in, while McCudden desperately extracted bullets for his rifle, one at a time from the jammed Lewis. More holes appeared as Johnson flew as fast as he could towards their own lines, where the German left them.

Coming in to land, some shell cases lodged under the joystick but Johnson cleared the obstruction in time to glide in safely.

After lunch, the same pilot went up again with a different observer, stalled his Morane soon after take-off and crashed. The observer was injured but recovered; Lieutenant Johnson was killed. Flying was a dangerous business.

James McCudden, with an English mother and Irish father, left school at 14, became a Post Office messenger boy and, as soon as he turned fifteen in 1910, joined the

Royal Engineers like his father. Dad was a sergeant major; son was a boy bugler, but elder brother William joined the Royal Flying Corps Military Wing and qualified as a sergeant pilot with No. 3 Squadron. Young James gave up bugling, trained as a mechanic and, posted to 3 Squadron at Netheravon, was soon scrounging a few unofficial flights with his brother.

Air Mechanic First Class McCudden went to France with No. 3 as the war began and was soon Sergeant McCudden. The death of brother William in a flying accident on 12 May 1915 deeply affected James but made him more determined than ever to play a significant role in this war. He volunteered for observer duties and had only a few trips in the summer as top mechanics were rarer than volunteer observers, but began flying regularly in the November. His devotion to duty and his observer adventures with Immelmann earned him the Croix de Guerre and, two days after his flight with Lieutenant Johnson, a posting to pilot training.

At Gosport, the first weeks of novice classes must have been a frustrating time for someone who knew all about aircraft and how they worked, could take one to pieces and put it back together, had flown many times over enemy lines and had had close encounters with the infamous Professor. Still, he had to go through the motions before taking to the air at last, on 22 February 1916, in a Farman F20, and qualifying by 16 April.

Even then the frustration continued. He had impressed his instructors so much that, instead of a posting to France, he had one as an instructor himself, and didn't get back to the war until June, with 20 Squadron flying

FE2B on offensive patrols and photo-reconnaissance, then to 29 Squadron flying the Airco DH2 fighter under the command of his old acquaintance Mr Conran, now a major. McCudden, still a sergeant, had his first victory on 9 September, when he shot down a two-seater.

Although in continuous action, sufficient to win him the Military Medal, his next kill didn't come until the new year. Now in the officers' mess as a second lieutenant, he was shot down himself, unhurt, on 23 January, and scored his second two-seater three days later. Over the next three weeks he had three more, one shared, before being brought home to instruct. Of this time, he said: 'I always wish I had had the advantage of a public school. After I joined the officers' mess I often felt ill at ease when the chaps were talking about things I didn't understand.'

In June and July of 1917, besides teaching, he also flew a Sopwith Pup, his first tractor fighter, in defensive sorties around London looking for German bombers.

His fighter-pilot career began in earnest in August 1917 when, as a captain and flight commander, he transferred to the much admired 56 Squadron, lately the home of famous ace Albert Ball VC (*q.v.*), flying the best fighter in the air at that time, the SE5A.

The first version of that machine, Scout Experimental 5, mainly designed by Henry Folland, was felt to be underpowered, by an unreliable engine, with an unreliable Vickers interruptor gear firing through the prop. The future author and BBC founder Cecil Lewis, said 'The SE5 as they turned it out was an abortion; it was the pilots of 56 Squadron who turned it into a practical fighter.' Lewis obviously played his part in that, shooting down eight

German aircraft in six weeks in said abortion, equipment unique to 56 Squadron.

Albert Ball, SE5 test pilot: 'The SE5 has turned out a dud. It's a great shame, for everybody expects such a lot from them. It is a rotten machine.' Having previously claimed thirty-two victories, the great majority in his favourite Nieuport 17, Ball had eleven such in the SE5A between 23 April and 5 May 1917. Not bad for a rotten machine.

The improved SE5A, with bigger engine, was the fastest thing around, at almost 140mph in level flight and sturdy enough to take a lot more in a dive. Pilots found it easier to fly than the Sopwith Camel and it was the better machine at high altitude. James McCudden later wrote: 'It was very fine to be in a machine that was faster than the Huns, and to know that one could run away just as things got too hot.'

With Ball dead, one of many on that squadron, and the SE5A proving itself, McCudden arrived to begin a fearsome series of kills, seven of the Albatros D5 in a row, and seventeen more assorted enemies.

Christmas time, 1917: while Biggles was stealing his turkey, history was being made in the freezing weather over St Quentin, home of 56 Squadron.

Having knocked down a DFW two-seater and damaged another on 22 December, Captain James McCudden took off on the 23rd at 10.30 hours in his SE5A, modified to his instructions so that he could climb faster and higher than specified. When flying as the lone hunter, he would get his height and hang around, waiting for German two-seaters to come a-photographing or nosing generally over the western, Entente side of the lines.

His first dish of the day was an LVG, tootling along. He waited until it was well into Entente territory, dived down, got behind, put in a short burst and saw steam and water issuing forth as the German descended gently to the east, back to his own country. The observer stood up, waving in apparent surrender, but the pilot persisted in heading homewards despite McCudden trying to push him west.

Surrender leading to escape was not part of the etiquette, so McCudden put in another burst of fire and watched the LVG dive out of control and crash just inside its own lines.

That fight had brought the British ace down to 6,000 feet, so he climbed back up again and spotted a Rumpler. This would not have been the common-or-garden Rumpler, the C1, which had a service ceiling of 16,500 feet, but the more advanced and unusual C4, which could reach 20,000 feet. It was said to fly well at that height although we can't imagine the pilot would like it much, or for long, in an open cockpit with no oxygen. Below that, McCudden was his enemy's equal.

In this case, the German fled with McCudden close behind. In defence, the Rumpler had to swerve to allow the gunner to fire without hitting his own tail, which slowed it down, allowing McCudden to come right in and shoot, removing both starboard wings.

This happened less than an hour after the LVG and was victim number thirty for McCudden. He saw two more LVG, attacked them without success and, low on petrol, went home for lunch.

Leading his patrol out in the afternoon, as they were

making their height he spotted a Rumpler, chased it, caught it and sent it down in a spiral. After an inconclusive battle between the patrol and a group of Albatros V-strutters, McCudden saw an LVG being fired on by archie. A signal from him stopped the archie and allowed him to fire instead, which resulted in the German flying sideways with the observer hanging on and trying to climb into the pilot's cockpit. The aircraft stalled, went into a spin, and fluttered down in autumn-leaf fashion, smashing into a train on a temporary light railway, knocking several trucks off the rails.

That was fourteen in December, including four totally destroyed in one day by one man. According to the RFC communiqué, that was the first time such a feat had been accomplished, which was true, to a point. Six months before, Raymond Collishaw (*q.v.*) had shot down four on 15 June in his Sopwith Tripehound, but they were not all confirmed destroyed and he was RNAS.

McCudden would do it again next year, on 8 February 1918, three destroyed and one captured, only to be outdone on 24 March 1918 by Captain John Lightfoot Trollope of 43 Squadron, aged twenty, in a Sopwith Camel, who shot down six in one day. This news would have affected McCudden not at all, unlike the notice he had of his younger brother's death in action. John McCudden MC, eight victories, had been shot down by Leutnant Ulrich Neckel (thirty victories), on 28 February 1918 but was not badly hurt. Flying again in his SE5A, he was killed on 18 March, becoming the first victim of Leutnant Hans Joachim Wolff (ten victories, killed 16 May 1918).

James Thomas Byford McCudden DSO and Bar, MC

and Bar, MM, Croix de Guerre, was sent home on 5 March 1918 as the top-scoring British ace with fifty-seven enemies confirmed defeated, and went to instruct at the aerial combat school in Scotland.

McCudden was being useful to the cause at fighter school but he always felt he could be more useful at the Front. A posting to France, for which he constantly agitated, would also get him away from the newspapers. He was called the 'Superman of the Air' by *The News of the World*, and how he hated it: 'I see the papers are making a fuss again about the ordinary things one does. Why, that's our work. Why fuss about it? I'm so tired of this limelight business. If only one could be left alone a bit more, and not so much of the hero about it.'

His wish was soon granted and, as Major McCudden, OC 60 Squadron, he set off for France in a new SE5A on 9 July 1918, and landed at an airfield at Auxi-le-Château, a small farming town not far from Abbeville. His destination, HQ 60 Squadron, was by a tiny hamlet five miles further on called Boffles, too small to be found easily. McCudden sought directions, took off as soon as he had them, and crashed inside two minutes.

His death was reported in *The Times* thus:

> The whole Air Service is in great grief at the loss of Major McCudden. His death was due to an inexplicable accident. He was on his way from Scotland to take up a new command, and flew over from England in his favourite single-seater. He landed successfully at one aerodrome in northern France, where he had business, and, after a short

stay set off again to join his squadron. While he was still only a few hundred feet from the ground his machine sideslipped and crashed among trees in the neighbourhood of the aerodrome. He was killed instantly.

The official record of his victories is 45 enemy aeroplanes brought down and 13 driven down. The quality of his flying was cool and deliberate judgment. He would manoeuvre patiently for position and keep it with astonishing skill and pertinacity till his enemy was shot down. No. man worked harder to make and maintain *esprit de corps* in his squadron. It was the squadron's record, not his own, that he chiefly cared for.

All true, almost. 'Where he had business' was nothing more than asking the way to Boffles, and he suffered a fractured skull in his crash, dying that night. His final accredited total of victories remained at fifty-seven.

Whether cause of death was pilot error, engine failure or a combination of the two, we shall never know. Witnesses said he made a sharp climbing turn, put the machine in a roll, lost height and went in.

Panicking error in a pilot like him is surely unlikely. His coolness and patience were legendary. He was certainly not a show-off and would never have tried to put on a circus trick. We must lean towards the conclusion that a serious fault in a new machine suddenly put him in a situation not even he could retrieve.

SUPPLEMENT

TO

The London Gazette

Of FRIDAY, the 29th of MARCH, 1918.

Published by Authority.

The Gazette is registered at the General Post Office for transmission by Inland Post as a newspaper. The postage rate to places within the United Kingdom, for each copy, is one halfpenny for the first 6 ozs., and an additional halfpenny for each subsequent 6 ozs. or part thereof. For places abroad the rate is a halfpenny for every 2 ounces, except in the case of Canada, to which the Canadian Magazine Postage rate applies.

TUESDAY, 2 APRIL, 1918.

War Office,
2nd April, 1918.

His Majesty the KING has been graciously pleased to approve of the award of the Victoria Cross to the undermentioned Officer :—

2nd Lt. (T./Capt.) James Byford McCudden, D.S.O., M.C., M.M., Gen. List and R.F.C.

For most conspicuous bravery, exceptional perseverance, keenness, and very high devotion to duty.

Captain McCudden has at the present time accounted for 54 enemy aeroplanes. Of these 42 have been definitely destroyed, 19 of them on our side of the lines. Only 12 out of the 54 have been driven out of control.

On two occasions he has totally destroyed four two-seater enemy aeroplanes on the same day, and on the last occasion all four machines were destroyed in the space of 1 hour and 30 minutes.

While in his present squadron he has participated in 78 offensive patrols, and, in nearly every case has been the leader. On at least 30 other occasions, whilst with the same squadron, he has crossed the lines alone, either in pursuit or in quest of enemy aeroplanes.

The following incidents are examples of the work he has done recently :—

On the 23rd December, 1917, when leading his patrol, eight enemy aeroplanes were attacked between 2.30 p.m. and 3.50 p.m. Of these two were shot down by Captain McCudden in our lines. On the morning of the same day he left the ground at 10.50 and encountered four enemy aeroplanes; of these he shot two down.

On the 30th January, 1918, he, single-handed, attacked five enemy scouts, as a result of which two were destroyed. On this occasion he only returned home when the enemy scouts had been driven far east; his Lewis gun ammunition was all finished and the belt of his Vickers gun had broken.

As a patrol leader he has at all times shown the utmost gallantry and skill, not only in the manner in which he has attacked and destroyed the enemy, but in the way he has during several aerial fights protected the newer members of his flight, thus keeping down their casualties to a minimum.

This officer is considered, by the record which he has made, by his fearlessness, and by the great service which he has rendered to his country, deserving of the very highest honour.

James McCudden's citation appeared on 29 March 1918.

GEORGES GUYNEMER, *LE BIEN-AIMÉ DE LA NATION*

Outscored only by René Fonck among French airmen, seventy-five victories to fifty-three, the frail, tubercular, diminutive Georges Marie Ludovic Jules Guynemer was a heart-throb among heart-throbs. Many of the top fliers became famous, in their enemies' countries as well as their own, but few were taken to a nation's heart like Guynemer.

Fonck, for instance, beyond whose record only von Richthofen could count, was seen as a bit of a braggart, one who gloried in his own magnificent record (quite the opposite of McCudden) and who liked to tell everybody about it. No, it was Georges who inspired the love of maidens (in the form of postal marriage proposals) and matrons (who wanted to mother him), who was mobbed by fans in the street, and who won the unlimited admiration of Frenchmen all. Not that he was unconscious of his talents; when told he was too young for the Légion d'Honneur, he noted drily that he was not too young to be shot at by Germans.

A contemporary of Alphonse Pégoud for a while, although not in the same escadrille, Corporal Guynemer had his first win on 19 July 1915, Morane Parasol versus Aviatik C. This made him a quick and determined starter as he'd only got his wings in the April, and that was after joining *l'Aéronautique Militaire* as an apprentice mechanic the previous November. And before that the army had turned him down as being physically unfit for duty.

According to his own report, Georges and his observer, Soldat Guerder, found the enemy machine on reconnaissance, its crew concentrating hard on their job, but surprise did not bring them immediate results:

Started with Guerder after a Boche reported at Couvres and caught up with him over Pierrefonds. Shot one belt, machine gun jammed, then unjammed. The Boche fled and landed in the direction of Laon. At Coucy we turned back and saw an Aviatik going toward Soissons at about 3200 metres up. We followed him, and as soon as he was within our lines we dived and placed ourselves about 50 metres under and behind him at the left. At our first salvo, the Aviatik lurched, and we saw a part of the machine crack. He replied with a rifle shot, one bullet hitting a wing, another grazing Guerder's hand and head. At our last shot the pilot sank down in the cockpit, the observer raised his arms, and the Aviatik fell straight downward in flames, into no-man's-land.

This might have been scored by the British as two victories, one driven off, one destroyed. Such events, shooting down and killing enemy flyers, were very rare in mid-1915, but the boy pilot and his mate were only awarded the Médaille Militaire, a middling kind of gong, like the (then new) Croix de Guerre, roughly equivalent to the British Mentioned in Despatches; but there were many more honours to come for Georges, and the general acclaim following this first victory made him famous in itself. Ace Jean Chaput (sixteen victories) had downed a Fokker Eindecker on 12 June, and the CO of Guynemer's next unit, Capitaine Félix Brocard, had also claimed a Boche but there was very little else to cheer about between Pégoud and our hero.

He was posted to Escadrille 3, known as *Les Cigognes* (storks on the squadron badge), commanded by Brocard but didn't score again for nearly half a year. His work was mostly reconnaissance, including several top-secret missions that had him landing behind enemy lines, which were noted in his later award as Chevalier de la Légion d'Honneur. Come September and the escadrille was re-equipping with the latest single-seater fighter, the Nieuport 11 Bébé, and Georges had half a dozen inconclusive combats in it, including one in which he and the German became locked briefly together, but the machine gun always seemed to jam at the most inconvenient moment.

His second conclusive victory has an extraordinary subplot. It was a Sunday, 5 December 1915 and, flying solo on patrol above his home town of Compiègne on the river Oise, Picardy, Georges spotted two enemy aircraft at 9,000 feet. He attacked one, an Aviatik C, closed in to 50 yards, fired, closed in to 20 yards, fired again and the German went down in a spin. Turning and searching for the second machine, which had disappeared meanwhile, he lost sight of his crashed victim and couldn't find it again.

Low on fuel, unable to spend too much time looking, he landed in a field close to his local church, knowing his parents would soon be walking home from mass. Sure enough, they appeared and, according to Guynemer, this conversation ensued:

'Father, I have lost my Boche.'

'You have lost your Boche?'

'Yes, a machine that I have shot down. I must return to my escadrille, but I don't want to lose him.'

Father had his instructions, to search the area around

the village of Bailly and the woods close by, the Bois Carré. Papa might have protested that it was 10 kilometres away but, with the help of some local military, the crash site was found. Because there were no independent witnesses, the victory was not initially credited to Guynemer and his promotion to sergeant did not compensate. Deeply piqued and blushing brightly, he said 'It doesn't matter. I will get another.'

And so he did, many others, starting with two more that year, one of those being a Fokker E shared with fellow pilot Bucquet. Although the authorities could not say he was much older, they gave him the Légion d'Honneur. This is the citation dated 24 December 1915: 'Pilot of great gallantry, a model of devotion to duty and courage. During the course of the past six months he has fulfilled two missions of a special nature requiring the highest spirit of self-sacrifice, and has engaged in thirteen aerial combats, of which two ended in the destruction in flames of the enemy aircraft.'

Ace status was won on 3 February 1916, followed within half an hour by his sixth (and nineteen more before the year's end). Here is his report from that day: 'Attacked LVG at 11.10 which replied with its machine gun. Fired 47 shots at 100 metres; the enemy machine dived swiftly down to its own lines, smoking. Lost to view at 500 metres from the ground. LVG attacked at 11.40 from behind, at 20 metres; it turned into a spin, dived, and I pursued it to 1300 metres, to see it fall 3 kilometres from Boche lines.'

Around this time, better German machines began to appear, single-seater fighters with powerful engines and fixed machine guns firing through the propeller, opposed to Guynemer's single gun on the top wing, and they introduced a new tactic of flying in small groups. Even so, Georges had his seventh and eighth wins before getting his first come-uppance, when a fight with a pair of opponents put holes in his aircraft and gave him many facial wounds, plus two bullets in his left arm. That was in March 1916, and he was out until May, returning to six more victories before his new aircraft arrived, the SPAD 7, in September. This machine was not so nimble as the Nieuport but was much faster,120mph-plus, 10,000 feet in 15 minutes, and so sturdy that it could dive at 200 mph without fear of disintegrating. It was a machine of great escapes as well as one of diving attacks out of the sun, at speeds unknown until then. Possibly the most welcome innovation was the Vickers .303 synchronised to fire through the prop.

In his SPAD, one of the first of this type to be allocated at the Front, Georges began with a couple of two-seater reconnaissance planes, then embarked on a remarkable series of nine single-seat German fighters, three Eindecker, three Albatros and three Halberstadt.

It might have been more: 'September 22: strangled a Fokker in 30 seconds that tumbled down disabled' but that was not accredited. Next day he had more satisfaction: 'Two combats near Eterpigny. At 11.20 forced down a Boche in flames near Aches; at 11.21 forced a Boche to land, damaged, near Carrépuy, passenger killed; at 11.25 forced down a Boche in flames near Roye.'

The two flamers were Eindecker. The two-seater was not accredited, but Georges' day was not over: 'At 11.30, was forced down myself by a French shell, and smashed my machine near Fescamps.'

The shell took away all the fabric from the port upper wing and put him into a tailspin, which he turned into a very fast diving glide, hitting the ground at about 100mph. He wrote to his father:

'Everything broken into matchwood. Nothing was left but the fuselage. The SPAD is strong; with any other machine I should now be thinner than this sheet of paper.'

The escadrille moved early in 1917 from the Somme to Lorraine, to a base near Nancy, partly to defend against bombing raids on that city. On 8 February 1917, one report has a massive flotilla of fifteen Gotha heavy bombers with fighter escorts heading for Nancy from Freiburg, which is surely unlikely as these must have been Gotha Mark 3. Only twenty-five were ever built and most of those were stationed on the Eastern Front, fighting in the Balkans. Anyway, Guynemer intercepted however many there were, attacked one of the lumbering giants from behind and, despite fire from the tail-gunner, forced it down with damaged engines. It crashed by the tiny village of Bouconville, in the Ardennes, with crew captured, and was taken to Nancy to be exhibited in the famous and impressively large Place Stanislas (see picture overleaf).

Something of a red-letter day was 16 March, when Georges downed three Boche (one shared), followed by another the next day, three more over the next few weeks, then four in one day, 25 May, two on 5 June, two on 7 July, with various singles in between, two on 17 August, and one DFW in a new SPAD 13 on 20 August. Perhaps

The Gotha was the first moderately successful German heavy bomber. In the prophetic words of Manfred von Richthofen: 'It seems not impossible that the day may come when a whole division will be transported in such a thing. In its body one can go for a walk. It contains an apparatus for wireless telephony by means of which one can converse with the people down below. At every corner is a gun. The whole thing is a flying fortress, and the planes with their stays and supports look like arcades. I have never been able to feel enthusiasm for these giant barges. I find them horrible, unsportsmanlike, boring and clumsy. I rather like a machine of the type of le petit rouge [nickname for his red-painted Fokker].'

motivated by the unwillingness of the authorities to credit him with all the victories he believed he deserved, he had a special camera made for him in Paris with which he expected to photograph his enemies as they fell.

His friends and family had begun to notice a change in him. Instead of the gay cavalier he seemed morbid on occasions, and was liable to come out with gnomic phrases. 'My fate is sealed, I cannot escape it.' '*Hodie mihi, cras tibi*' – 'Today [victory is] to me, tomorrow to you.' 'I have my bag of fifty Boche.'

His own SPAD 7 was in dock. After a string of frustrating, failed attacks, usually due to mechanical imperfections all blamed on flying a different machine, everyone could see a man at the end of his tether. His tuberculosis was nagging at him. He was suffering from combat fatigue and the aerial equivalent of shell shock. Any senior officer would have at least forced him to take some leave, but his CO had been wounded and had not yet been replaced.

As it was, on 11 September Guynemer took off in his own machine, not yet properly flight-tested or, according to other stories, a SPAD 13. The latter perhaps makes more sense as his last victory had been in one of that marque. In any case, he was with Sous-lieutenant Bozon-Verduraz on a patrol. The pair of pilots found nothing until they were over the ruined remnants of Poelkapelle, not far from Ypres, where they spied a two-seater below. Guynemer's first diving attack missed, so he came again and again, chasing the dodging German lower and lower while, of course, the enemy fired back.

Bozon-Verduraz was distracted by the appearance of a flight of single-seaters. There was no sign of his beloved Georges when he returned to the scene.

German reports stated that the great man was brought down from 2,000 feet into Poelkapelle, by Leutnant Kurt Wissemann of Jasta 3, a very successful single-seater fighter unit equipped with Halberstadt and Albatros. Wissemann's record shows his claim for a SPAD 13 at 10.30 on the day in question, in the right place, as his fifth victory. It was his last too, as he was killed two weeks later.

On the ground, there was time only to identify Guynemer's body, noting that he had been shot through the head, before Entente artillery bombardment forced the investigators away. Subsequent shelling destroyed machine and body completely.

Médaille Militaire, Croix de Guerre with twenty-six palms, Distinguished Service Order from the British, Belgian Order of Léopold II, Chevalier de la Légion d'Honneur, Officier de la Légion d'Honneur, Russian

The man himself in heroic pose.'Remember that until one has given all, one has given nothing.'

Cross of St George, these and more were the footnotes to something like six hundred aerial combats, being shot down seven times himself, fifty-three Boche victims and probably more.

Ernst Udet (*q.v.*) said it all, after he came off second best against Guynemer in May or June 1917: 'Not only the machine above me is better, but the man sitting in it can do more than I.'

FREDERICK LIBBY, ACE COWBOY

Fred Libby is usually given as the first American ace. He certainly was the first American to become an ace before he ever flew an aeroplane in war.

Young Fred really had been a cowboy in Arizona and he really did know how to use a gun, but he came to the war via Canada, long before there was any American involvement. Driving a truck in the mud and rain of the Western Front, he volunteered for the RFC as an observer and, according to him, had a morning's training on machine guns and was up in the afternoon.

After a few hours' aerial practice he went on his first patrol, observer in Lieutenant E D Hicks's FE2B pusher. They came across an unusual enemy, the AGO C2 reconnaissance aircraft, also a pusher with a gunner sitting in the front, but with a twin-boom fuselage. The FE2B was no faster than the AGO, indeed it was probably a bit slower, so the only advantage the RFC had was the American sharpshooter behind the .303. The German went down in flames.

Libby was posted from 23 Squadron to 11 Squadron,

where he was crewed with Captain Stephen Price who was a flight commander but had, so far, no victories. With cowboy Fred in the front seat, Price had three in one day, 22 August, and four more before he was transferred to home defence.

Of course this made Fred an ace too, if you counted the victories as his, which strictly speaking they didn't. He scored with two other 11 Squadron pilots as well, taking him up to ten, before completing his pilot training and moving to 43 Squadron in April 1917 and the Sopwith 1½ Strutter. This was an unusual machine, the first two-seater tractor fighter. It had a fixed machine gun with synchro gear firing through the prop, and the observer in the rear seat had a full field of fire with his gun.

The Sopwith Strutter was the first British aircraft in the war offering a forward-firing gun with propeller synchronisation. Various synchro systems were tried but all of the early ones required a certain amount of luck.

Drawbacks included a not entirely reliable synchro, and the new German fighters entirely outclassing it by this time. Fred arrived in the middle of the worst month the squadron ever had, known as Bloody April, when No. 43's casualties were equivalent to its whole officer establishment of thirty-two. Fred was an officer too, with the Military Cross for his gunnery feats, and he managed two victories as pilot in his Sopwith, a two-seater and an Albatros D3 'straight-winged' machine, before transferring again, to 25 Squadron and the DH4.

This aircraft was a high-performance bomber, 140 mph-plus, a fast climber with ceiling at over 20,000 feet, carrying 460lb of bombs. It was able to outfly most German fighters and could fight back, like the Sopwith, with guns fore and aft. The tasks were long-range reconnaissance and bombing, but as a flight commander Fred still managed to fit in two more scores including an Albatros D5.

His four victories as pilot do not qualify him as an ace, but his ten more as top gun surely allow him his place in the American book of heroes, a pre-eminence celebrated in style by the newspapers when he was called back home to instruct in the hastily reorganising and expanding US Air Service.

The *Kansas City Star* had him bringing down twelve Huns in the first months of 1917, making twenty-two altogether, all apparently as a pilot. The *Ohio Repository* did differentiate between observer and pilot victories but still gave him twenty-two, and said: 'It is unlikely that a better man could be found for the work of training the young flyers who are being sent to the Front.'

Albert Ball's film-star looks and dashing achievements in the air made him the first RFC pilot to become a national celebrity, and, more than that, an unusually glamorous symbol of the national spirit.

ALBERT BALL, MATINEE IDOL VC

Albert Ball came from an upwardly mobile family; father went from plumber to Sir Albert, Lord Mayor of Nottingham. Albert was not blessed academically, but he offered several talents that could be useful as a First World War flyer. He was a crack shot, with superb eyesight, and he was more than competent with engines.

The actual flying bit did not come easily at first and his trainers marked him as average and sometimes worse. He was deeply religious and something of an introvert, so fitting in with life in the officers' mess did not look likely.

Like almost every pilot then, he began on general duties, flying reconnaissance ops in a BE2C. After a couple of no-result fights, being shot down by archie and having a go at a balloon, Ball's combative spirit was recognised and he was given a Bristol Scout to fly, at that time the superior beast to the Eindecker. He had his first victory in that, then swapped to a Nieuport 16, then a 17. During this time, the summer of 1916, he had a mysterious posting for a month to a recco squadron, but was back to fighters by mid-August and knocked down nine Huns in the rest of that month, taking him to seventeen, and by the end of September he was on thirty-one.

None of his victories was shared; he much preferred flying alone, his commanders mostly permitted it, and he never shied away no matter what the odds in numbers of enemies.

A period of home leave allowed him to spend Christmas with his family and meet an eighteen-year-old girl, Flora Young. He took her up in a plane, proposed, she accepted, and they were to have married on his next home leave.

Also during that time he'd been asked to test the new fighter, the SE5. He didn't like it: too heavy on the controls. Luckily, his view was not widely shared and that machine became a legend, partly because of Ball himself. Returning to France, he was a flight commander with 56 Squadron, flying the SE5A. He had ten more victories in that marque, including two in a day four times.

The Red Baron's Flying Circus was the talk of the Front by now; Ball was desperate to deal it a mighty blow and was planning a special op against it when he got his chance. He ran into Jasta 11, led by Manfred von Richthofen's brother Lothar, on 7 May 1917. There was a big fight in darkening skies and Ball was last seen flying into cloud, possibly in pursuit of a Fokker Triplane, possibly von Richthofen's. As to what happened next, one certainty is the falsity of the German claim, that Lothar had shot down Albert Ball (listed as his number twenty. Final score forty minus one, including six more British aces).

Ball had no bullet wounds and his aircraft showed no battle damage sufficient to bring it down. He died from injuries suffered in his crash, which was very likely caused by engine failure.

Lauded to the heavens as the epitome of the true British, God-fearing hero, at least one newspaper man, who had actually met him at his parents' house, remembered to mention his often expressed dislike of killing, his preference for his own company and, perhaps most remarkable of all in that super-high energy, taut-nerved world, the little garden that he cultivated on the airfield.

There is no doubt that he went into battle filled with something of that spiritual fervour

---

Lt. (temp. Capt.) Albert Ball, D.S.O., M.C., late Notts. and Derby. R., and R.F.C.

For most conspicuous and consistent bravery from the 25th of April to the 6th of May, 1917, during which period Capt. Ball took part in twenty-six combats in the air and destroyed eleven hostile aeroplanes, drove down two out of control, and forced several others to land.

In these combats Capt. Ball, flying alone, on one occasion fought six hostile machines, twice he fought five and once four. When leading two other British aeroplanes he attacked an enemy formation of eight. On each of these occasions he brought down at least one enemy.

Several times his aeroplane was badly damaged, once so seriously that but for the most delicate handling his machine would have collapsed, as nearly all the control wires had been shot away. On returning with a damaged machine he had always to be restrained from immediately going out on another.

In all, Capt. Ball has destroyed forty-three German aeroplanes and one balloon, and has always displayed most exceptional courage, determination and skill.

Albert Ball VC, DSO and Two Bars, MC, forty-four victories, twenty-one years of age, never saw the citation for his Victoria Cross, which appeared in the *London Gazette* on 8 June 1917. He had already been dead a month.

which possessed the old Crusaders. Young as he was, and by no means given to philosophic or religious reflection, there are in between the sporting phrases of his letters, typical of a public schoolboy, devout references to his God. He was conscious of a Divine Presence that dwelt with him in his flights in the heavens and in the merciless combats with his foes. 'Re saying a few words to God when doing my work and when it is done,' he wrote to his parents. 'You ask me if I do when I get back safely. You bet I do; I even do when I am fighting; and in fact I put all my trust in God. In His hands I feel safe no matter in what mess I get.'

H Russell Stannard, writing in *The Weekly Despatch* (later known as *The Sunday Despatch*), 4 November 1917.

MICK MANNOCK, SOCIALIST PATRIOT

Edward Corringham 'Mick' Mannock began his war in a Turkish jail, interned from his job with the Istanbul telephone company as an enemy alien. Under the harsh regime his health deteriorated; the Turks decided he was an unnecessary burden, being unfit for military duty, and sent him home. Recovered, he joined the Medical Corps, transferred to the Royal Engineers, learned to fly, and thence to the RFC for advanced training under James McCudden.

He joined 40 Squadron in France in April 1917, flying the Nieuport 17, the bigger, faster, altogether better development of the Bébé, at the time the best Entente fighter although, in the RFC, still with the wingtop gun. Mannock had personal difficulties, similar to those felt by McCudden. Most RFC officers were indeed 'officer class', not working class, Labour Party boys of Irish parentage like Mannock, and his social uncertainty made him seem aloof. It didn't help when he told the other officers just how the war, society and everything else should be reorganised, nor did it go down well when he openly admitted the fears that the others kept to themselves. He was frequently sick before flying on operations, and he didn't start well in the mess when, on his first day, he unknowingly sat in the customary chair of an officer who had been killed that afternoon.

Beginning with a balloon on May 7, Mick Mannock had sixteen victories with 40 Squadron, mostly Albatros D5 fighters and DFW C5 reconnaissance machines, before being withdrawn from the Front in the new year, by which time he was Captain Mannock MC and Bar and a flight commander, despite the feeling among some fellow officers that he wasn't really suitable for seniority.

In a training role with 74 Squadron, he lectured on aerial combat and became known as a charismatic and highly effective teacher, formulating a set of practical rules for air fighting on the Western Front that went beyond Boelcke's *Dicta*:

You must dive to attack with zest and hold your fire until you get within a hundred yards of your target. Achieve surprise by approaching from the east (as it were from the German lines), using sun and cloud to avoid being seen and, 'Gentlemen, always above; seldom on the same level; never underneath'.

Practice is supremely important, in making quick turns, in shooting and range-finding, aircraft recognition at long distance, flying in different weather, time-keeping in the air, and in exercise to keep fit.

Treat every aeroplane as an enemy until you are sure it is not. Know where the enemy's blind spots are. Beware of decoys; if you see a single enemy machine, search the sky above before attacking.

Keep turning in a dog fight; never fly straight except when firing, and never dive away from an enemy. Bullets fly faster than aeroplanes.

Mannock was a great motivator, and his students put their knowledge and enthusiasm into use when the squadron moved to France on 30 March equipped with the SE5A. Over the next four months, Mannock ramped up his official tally to fifty-two, including seven shared, scoring two in a day seven times, three in a day twice, and four in a day once. The citation to his DSO Second Bar stated:

This officer has now accounted for 48 enemy machines. His success is due to wonderful shooting and a determination to get to close quarters; to attain this he displays most skilful leadership and unfailing courage. These characteristics were markedly shown on a recent occasion when he attacked six hostile scouts, three of which he brought down. Later on the same day he attacked a two-seater, which crashed into a tree.

Mannock replaced the Canadian Major William Bishop as CO of 85 Squadron in early July and set about restoring morale and team spirit, which had somewhat dissipated under the controversial ace. Leading from the front, he scored nine more victories, including a two-in-a-day and a three-in-a-day. On the 26th of that month he took with him on patrol a young New Zealander, Lieutenant Donald Inglis, who had yet to shoot down a German. They, or possibly Mannock alone, destroyed a Hannover C reconnaissance/fighter machine but were themselves hit by ground fire on the way back to St Omer.

Inglis staggered home; Mannock fell in flames. By this time he had MC and Bar, DSO and two Bars. His VC was awarded posthumously and not until a year later, well after the war was over, which was possibly because he had somehow escaped much of the media attention lavished on other high scorers such as McCudden and Albert Ball.

It has been said that this was a man who truly hated the enemy and delighted in his kills, but he was more complex than that. He was a fierce patriot who had to conquer his private dreads and terrors, especially of being burned alive, before he could send others along that particular potential route to hell.

His final number of victories is uncertain, largely because he was not meticulous about reporting them, and the number sixty-one should probably be higher, and with some more shared victories. In any case, Major Mick Mannock was the highest scoring British ace, four ahead of 'Mac' McCudden.

MAJ. EDWARD MANNOCK IS NAMED CHAMPION FLIER LONDON, May 4 1919 (British Wireless Service) The Air Ministry has decided that, so far as can be ascertained, the champion British airman of the war was the late Major Edward Mannock. Lieutenant-Colonel William A Bishop, the Canadian aviator, who won the Victoria Cross, comes next. Mannock brought down seventy-three enemy machines and Bishop seventy-two. Of all the allies, Lieutenant René Fonck, the French ace, holds the record with seventy-eight.

The late Baron Richthofen of German 'flying circus' fame, claimed to hold the world's record for the number of machines he had destroyed, but the Germans worked on a different system respecting official confirmation of each victory, and his record has not been confirmed.

Indeed, the Germans did work on a different system, as mentioned earlier, with more stringent criteria. Confirmation has come with subsequent research. Actual scores were: von Richthofen eighty, Fonck seventy-five, Bishop seventy-two, Udet sixty-two, Mannock sixty-one.

Regardless of scores, Mannock's VC citation stated his best claim to fame: 'This highly distinguished officer, during the whole of his career in the Royal Air Force, was an outstanding example of fearless courage, remarkable skill, devotion to duty and self-sacrifice, which has never been surpassed.'

Bob Little, here in naval uniform, was the highest scoring Australian pilot with forty-seven victories.

BOB LITTLE, TOP AUSSIE SAILOR

As well as their specifically naval aeronautics and their home-defence roles, the Royal Naval Air Service had fighter squadrons on the Western Front. Because of their special contractual relationship with the Sopwith company, these squadrons were usually the first to be supplied with the new Sopwith fighters as they came out, the Pup, the Triplane and the Camel. The squadrons, Nos 1, 3, 4, 8, 9 and 10, counted well over a hundred aces between them, including one of the top men of all, Raymond Collishaw (q.v.) with sixty victories, and the highest scoring Australian airman, Robert Alexander Little with forty-seven.

Bob Little came from Hawthorn, Melbourne, Victoria. Along with hundreds of other applicants, he couldn't get into the very small Australian army flying school, so he sailed for England determined to learn to fly even if he had to pay for it himself, which he did, and joined the RNAS at nineteen. His first posting in June 1916 was to a Strutter flight in Dunkirk, flying bombing raids, but he was switched to fighters in October when the newly formed 8 Squadron arrived in France with the latest Sopwith machine, the Pup.

Meanwhile he had done something unusual for a twenty-year-old, which was to take some Blighty leave in order to marry. This was not the normal thing for pilots of that war, knowing their likely lifespan, and it was to a girl he'd only known a short while, Vera Field from Dover. Well, that was Bob Little. As one of his commanding officers, Raymond Collishaw, would say of him later, 'Bold, aggressive and courageous, yet he was gentle and kindly'.

Little's first four victories were described in his citation for the DSC (Distinguished Service Cross, Royal Navy equivalent of DFC):

> For conspicuous bravery in successfully attacking and bringing down hostile machines on several occasions. On 11th November, 1916, he attacked and brought down a hostile machine in flames. On 12th December, 1916, he attacked a German machine at a range of 50 yards; this machine was brought down in a nose-dive. On 20th December, 1916, he dived at a hostile machine, and opened fire at 25 yards range; the observer was seen to fall down inside the machine, which went down in a spinning nose-dive. On 1st January, 1917, he attacked an enemy scout, which turned over on its back and came down completely out of control.

The RFC had some 365 aircraft, two-thirds reconnaissance two-seaters, one third fighters, in support of the army at Arras, in April 1917. The Germans had the new Albatros D fighters; the RFC had FE8 and DH2 pushers, plus the now inferior Pups and Nieuports. It was carnage. In that single month the RFC lost almost 250 machines, with most crew killed or captured. It was Bloody April all right and yet, in that same month, Bob Little, flying the new Sopwith Triplane, had eight victories including five Albatros D3. The other RNAS squadrons with the Tripehound, Nos 1, 9 and 10, had similar success but this machine and the other new fighter, the SPAD 7, were in short supply elsewhere.

The Sopwith Triplane was not much faster than its opponents and it usually had one Lewis gun while the Albatros D3 had twin Spandau, but having three sets of wings rather than two gave it shorter span but increased area, which in turn meant a new standard of manoeuvrability and climb rate. It could reach 10,000 feet in ten minutes. So long as German speeds stayed where they were, the Tripehound was always favourite in a fight, which impressed the Germans enough for them to develop their own Fokker Triplane that the Red Baron liked so much.

Little's April performance brought him a Bar to his DSC, and he did something similar in May, with eight more, six of them Albatros D3, and the medals were coming as fast as his victories. His DSO recognised his achievements to the end of June, and the citation for his Bar to that high order described his activities in July, fourteen victories, with two in a day three times.

Although a social animal in the mess and good company, he preferred being his own man in the air where he could make his Tripe do tricks in dogfights that no Albatros could equal. He was also a consummate marksman and could outshoot just about anyone at a moving target, but there were many pilots on both sides who had better mastered some of the basics, such as landing an aircraft without damaging it. Even in his junior days, one superior officer reported: 'He has a trick of landing outside the aerodrome.'

By mid-July he was flying Camels, no faster than the Tripe but even more aerobatic and, in the right hands, near unbeatable, which was just as well as he was now meeting the Albatros D5. Not that it made much difference to Bob Little. His ten Camel victories included five D5.

As August began, Little was up to thirty-eight wins out of a great many more combats, and he was due a rest. The Admiralty had recently decided that a new aerodrome was needed at home, from which to defend shipping, and the site chosen was Hawkshill Down at Walmer, near Deal in Kent. The policy was to recruit the flying establishment from France, to give the hardest working, most successful RNAS pilots a few months of relatively easy, low stress duty after the boiling mayhem of the Western Front. Bob Little was one such recruit, and his R&R included a period of normal family life with wife Vera and young son.

He could have stayed there or taken a desk job somewhere but of course that wouldn't do. He agitated for a posting back to France and in April 1918, Captain Little, flight commander, arrived just as No. 3 Squadron RNAS became 203 Squadron Royal Air Force. Flying Sopwith

Camels again, he had five victories in eleven days. On 21
April he shot down a Pfalz fighter and then this happened:

> I was attacked by six other enemy aircraft which
> drove me down through the formation below
> me. I spun but had my controls shot away and
> my machine dived. At 100 ft from the ground it
> flattened out with a jerk, breaking the fuselage
> just behind my seat. I undid the belt and when
> the machine struck the ground I was thrown
> clear. The EA still fired at me while I was on the
> ground. I fired my revolver at one which came
> down to about 30 ft. They were driven off by rifle
> and machine gun fire from our troops.

Claiming Little as his victory was Friedrich Ehmann, eight
victories in his Pfalz, one of whom was another Aussie
ace, Richard Pearman Minifie, twenty-one victories – and
he didn't manage to kill him either.

There were three more Germans for Bob Little before the
almost inevitable happened and, as is so often the way, we
know the result but not the details. He took off on the night
of 27 May from Treizennes aerodrome near Ayr-sur-la-Lys
in the Pas de Calais, looking for Gotha bombers reported
in the area.

He was found next morning, dead in his machine from
a wound to the groin, near Nœux-les-Mines (Béthune, Pas
de Calais). Following an agreement they had made, his
young wife took their toddler son to Melbourne and made
a home on the same street as her husband's parents.

WILLY COPPENS, KING BUSTER

Observation balloons were vital tools of reconnaissance. From their wicker basket suspended beneath the gas bag at, say, 3,500 feet, the crew of two could see a single soldier on the ground five miles away and a lorry ten miles away. Their main jobs were to spot for the artillery and to report on troop movements but they also relayed the news about anything interesting and/or unusual in this largely static war. Early in the war they communicated by semaphore flags, but they soon had wireless sets.

Balloons were always important targets for both sides, but especially so before infantry attacks when enemy spying had to be kept to a minimum. For airmen, trying to destroy balloons was a risky business. There would

The British began the war with spherical balloons but soon switched to the more aerodynamic designs like this one. They were big, fat, stationary targets and tended to become a specialisation for certain airmen.

be archie in strength, possibly fighter escorts, and you had to be quick. Balloons were on motorised winches so they could be pulled down rapidly and, being filled with hydrogen, you had to be careful not to get too involved in your own success. Ordinary machine gun bullets were largely ineffective as they just went straight through, so dedicated balloon busters carried incendiary ammunition.

The crews carried no defences but did have parachutes, of a sufficiently primitive design to produce an interesting quandary. As soon as enemy aircraft appeared the crew would want to jump, because it was impossible to do so from a burning balloon and they were sitting ducks anyway in their basket, but the chute might not work. There was no equivalent to the modern chute, or the types used in the Second World War, easily portable and simply deployed. The main part of a balloonist's parachute was slung over the side of the basket in a sack, linked to the crewman's harness by a cord. When he jumped, he hoped that the cord would pull the chute out of its bag. Even when the chute opened properly, there was still the danger of machine gun bullets from the attackers, and of burning debris from above.

Despite all this, they were much better than the alternative and were well used. On one occasion, on 6 October 1918, a single American balloon was attacked four times, forcing the crew to jump twice, and one of those crewmen, a Lieutenant McDevitt, had made a jump the day before.

The expert balloon busters were mostly French and German. The highest scoring Britisher was Camel pilot

Henry Woollett DSO, MC and Bar, with eleven balloons (none shared) out of thirty-five victories but his speciality was the Albatros D5, including six in one day, on 12 April 1918. Highest scoring RFC man was South African Andrew Beauchamp-Proctor VC, DSO, DFC, MC and Bar, sixteen out of fifty-four, three shared, all scored from his SE5A.

Top German was Friedrich Ritter von Röth, twenty balloons out of twenty-eight victories, none shared. He began balloon-busting after two years of hospital treatment for infantry wounds and flying injuries, with three on 28 January 1918, plus three on 1 April, five on 29 May, three on 13 August, three on 10 October and the other three in between. He committed suicide after the war (see 'Last Men Down' page 235)

Maurice Boyau, captain of the French rugby team in the 1913 Five Nations championships, had twenty-one out of thirty-five, fourteen balloon victories shared. He was killed towards the end of the war, on 16 September, burning his last balloon but claimed as the fourteenth victory of twenty-five by Leutnant Georg von Hantelmann.

Michel Coiffard had twenty-four out of thirty-four, twenty-one of his balloons shared, victories numbers four to twenty-five won in six weeks of 1918. He was wounded four times serving in the infantry, and died of wounds suffered while winning his last victory, a Fokker D7, on 28 October 1918.

Léon Bourjade took time off from his training for the priesthood to claim twenty-seven balloons out of twenty-eight, fifteen of the balloons shared victories. He later died taking the word of the Lord to the people of New Guinea.

The king of all balloon busters has to be Belgian Willy Coppens, thirty-five out of thirty-seven, none shared, his two other victories being two-seaters, and all of them in his Hanriot HD1 single-seater fighter. This was a French machine, never flown in anger by the French but highly favoured by the Belgians and Italians. It was small, very nimble, not as fast as some but sturdy and reliable and very manoeuvrable, entering service during the summer of 1917.

Willy Omer François Jean Coppens de Houthulst, from Watermael-Boitsfort (Watermaal-Bosvoorde), now a suburb on the south-east side of Brussels, joined the army in 1912 and transferred to the Belgian air service in 1915. He wasn't 'de Houthulst' then; such an extra name

denotes a Belgian knighthood, which was bestowed on him for his wartime feats.

At his own expense, he was one of forty Belgians to enrol at Hendon flying school. There was some further official training, before he began flying two-seaters on reconnaissance missions in 1916. Perhaps it was in this period that he had his Damascene moment and knew he had to get into fighters and shoot down those Boche in their

Willy Coppens, king of the balloon busters, and champion of the single-seater Hanriot HD1 favoured by the Belgian air force.

Drachen (literally dragons but actually meaning kite, or toy floating in the air on a string), as they were called.

He was a bit of a showman, our Willy, and liked to make a flying display after busting a balloon, for the benefit of any watching Germans. On one famous occasion, he was greatly disconcerted to see his dragon coming up at him instead of going down, fast enough to take him and his Hanriot with it. Stranded on this inflatable landing ground, he had to wait until it tilted enough to let him slide off, luckily before it caught fire.

With less than a month of the war left, Coppens was busting number thirty-seven when he took a bullet in his left leg, causing enough damage to make amputation necessary after a hurried crash-landing.

After the war he took up parachuting, something he could never have done as a serving pilot although he must have seen plenty of Boche doing it as he roared up to his next Drachen. In 1928 he set a world record that lasted for four years, by jumping from almost 20,000 feet.

FRANCESCO BARACCA, HANSA-BRANDENBURG *INTENDITORE*

Every air force had a workhorse, and the Austro-Hungarians' general-purpose reconnaissance/bomber was the Hansa-Brandenburg C, designed by Ernst Heinkel. Like the British RE8 and the German Albatros, the French Dorand and Salmson and the Italian Pomilio, these two-seaters came out of the realisation after war began that something more than an unarmed kite was required. The Hansa-Brandenburg did not have outstanding performance,

The RFC's workhorses were the BE2C and, shown here, the RE8. This 9 Squadron example lasted two weeks in August 1917. Two-seater armed reconnaissance/ general purpose machines like this included the Austrian Hansa-Brandenburg, the German Albatros and the Italian Pomilio.

top speed 80mph, but it did the job. Unlike the others mentioned, it had a single, two-seat cockpit rather than two separate offices.

When Italy declared for the Entente with war on Austria on 24 May 1915, few interested parties outside of those two old enemies took very much notice. Half the Italian army wasn't ready to advance and, in any case, the Alps were in the way. Most of the fighting happened to the east, along the river Isonzo (modern Slovenia) that ran beside the Austrian/ Italian border, and the coastal plains around there.

Near the ancient city of Udine was based a cavalry officer turned pilot, Francesco Baracca, whose No. 8 Squadron was equipped with the Nieuport 10. This machine was a two-seater jeep that they tried to convert to a fighter, with a gun on the top wing, but it was pretty hopeless and no Italians managed to shoot down any Austrians in one.

In April 1916, the Nieuport 11 Bébé arrived on the Udine/ Isonzo Front, also with a gun on the top wing but purpose-made as a fighter, smaller, single-seat, much faster and much more agile. Baracca was delighted. If the machine gun on this Bébé didn't jam as often as in his previous abortive attacks, maybe Francesco would have a chance.

His first victory was the first of any Italian, on 7 April 1916, a Hansa-Brandenburg C1, damaging it, wounding the crew and forcing it to land. Another came in May, a Lohner B7, the sometimes unarmed version of the long-range reconnaissance machine made by the Viennese coachbuilder Lohner, a firm known for horseless carriages designed by Ferdinand Porsche.

Victims were widely spaced that summer and autumn, with two Hansa-Brandenburg C and one Lloyd C3, another 80mph reconnaissance two-seater, but Francesco really got going in 1917 as the Hansa-Brandenburg connoisseur, starting on New Year's Day with the first of a run of fourteen of that type up to 6 September, during which he re-equipped with the 110mph Nieuport 17, then the 120mph SPAD 7.

One of those Hansas was piloted by Austro-Hungarian ace Julius Busa, who must have been blessed with a top-class observer because all his five victories were won from Lloyd and Hansa machines but, obviously, not good enough for Baracca in his SPAD.

Eleven more victories in the year included only two of his favourite target, plus seven of the DFW C5 two-seater, a much better machine than the near-obsolete Hansa. He also had two of the excellent German-built fighter Albatros D3, one of them flown by Hungarian ace Oberleutnant Rudolf Szepessy-Sokoll (five victories).

Baracca had a prancing black horse painted on all his earlier aircraft as a tribute to his cavalry background. Sports car enthusiasts might recognise it as the symbol of Ferrari, and that is indeed where it came from.

After another Hansa and an Albatros D in May 1918, the Italian ace, now a national hero, upgraded again to the SPAD 13 and on 15 June took down a similar pair, bringing him to a score of thirty-four.

There are several versions of Baracca's end. The two reported in the newspapers at the time were that he shot himself rather than endure captivity and/or being burned to death, or that he was brought down by ground fire. Certainly he was on a strafing mission, flying low over Austrian troops, and he had a bullet wound in his head and, according to one source, his service revolver in his hand.

Baracca's defeat was also claimed as one of the four credited to an Austrian two-seater pilot, Max Kauer of *Fliegerkompagnie* 28, although the Italian's wingman on this op, Franco Osnago, did not mention seeing any enemy aircraft.

However he died, Francesco Baracca's life at war was rewarded with the Medaglia d'Oro al Valore Militare, gold medal, equivalent to the Victoria Cross, three of the Medaglia d'Argento, silver, equivalent to the MC, plus an actual Military Cross, the Croix de Guerre with Palms and the Belgian Order of the Crown.

RAYMOND COLLISHAW – SHOT SIXTY AND LIVED

Raymond Collishaw was a first-generation Canadian, born of a Welsh family on Vancouver Island in 1893. His route to navy flying school at Redcar, North Riding of Yorkshire, was via the Royal Canadian Navy's fisheries protection service, in which he rose from cabin boy to first officer. First RNAS posting was to a home-defence squadron flying Strutters, thence to France and bombing raids on Germany. He had his first two scores on the same

Raymond Collishaw's flying circus of Tripehounds was led by this one, his own Black Maria.

day, 25 October 1916, knocking down two fighters near Lunéville.

From the Strutter he changed briefly to the Pup and 3 Squadron, where he had his third and fourth victories, and then began his purple patch, as a flight commander with 10 Squadron and the Triplane. He formed his own small circus, the Black Flight, with four more Canadians flying Tripes painted black and each named. Collishaw flew Black Maria. Ellis Reid of Toronto had Black Roger, J E Sharman of Winnipeg had Black Death, Gerald Nash of Hamilton was in Black Sheep, and Melville Alexander, Toronto, was the Black Prince.

Collishaw downed enemy aircraft on the 1st, 2nd, 3rd and 4th of June 1917, two on the 5th, and three on the 6th, when the Black Flight scored ten altogether. He had four in one day, 15 June, but lost Nash on the 25th when he was forced down behind enemy lines and captured, after a battle with a somewhat grander circus, von Richthofen's.

Collishaw became the first ace on either side to claim six victims in one day, 6 July, all Albatros D5. His DSC had already been announced, and he had the DSO, on 11 August, but by then he was crossing the Atlantic, sailing home to Canada on leave, having finished his tour of duty with two Albatros D5 on 27 July, making a total of thirty-eight.

He was back in November, commanding a flight of Sopwith Camels on escort duties with 13 Squadron based at St Pol, Dunkirk, protecting the navy's seaplanes on anti-shipping and land bombing raids. One more German was added to the list before Collishaw's posting on 23 January back to his old outfit, 3 Squadron, as CO, which meant no operational flying.

He had to put up with this ban, through his translation to CO of 203 Squadron RAF and on to June, when at last he could get back into a Camel and harry the Hun. He restarted his career with two Pfalz fighters on 11 June and carried on with a series of those and the new Fokker D7. He always maintained that dogfights between scouts were a sideshow compared to the really important work, which was artillery observation, reconnaissance, bombing, and convoy patrol, so no doubt he was pleased with his tally of five two-seaters in July. With the war almost over and the DFC and a Bar to his DSO awarded in rapid succession, he returned to England on 21 October 1918 with his score at sixty.

There was one more adventure to come, with volunteers in 47 Squadron fighting with the White Russians against the revolutionaries. The squadron was mixed, bombers and fighter-escorts; Captain Collishaw, one Nieuport destroyed, 9 October 1919, near Czaritsyn, or Stalingrad and Volgograd as it became known.

Air Vice-Marshal Raymond Collishaw CB, DSO and Bar, OBE, DSC, DFC, Croix de Guerre plus various Russian medals, retired from the RAF in 1943 and died in 1976 aged 82.

ERNST UDET, SHOT SIXTY-TWO AND LIVED

Ernst Udet is usually listed as the fourth highest scorer of the war, behind von Richthofen, Bishop and Fonck but, because of German efficiency in keeping records, we can be fairly sure that his true place is second. He had sixty-two confirmed victories, of which twenty came in one month, August 1918. He had two in a day eight times, and three in a day twice, beginning way back in March 1916 in a Fokker Eindecker. Towards the end of the war he was bringing down numbers of SE5A and Sopwith Camel in a Fokker D7, so he had seen pretty well all the process of fighter development.

He had also experienced all the process of fighter-pilot development, from the frozen incompetence of the terrified novice, to the cool brilliance of the supreme expert. The frozen incompetence happened in December 1915, with nineteen-year-old Udet in a Fokker Eindecker and a French crew of two in a Caudron G4 bomber, which was a twin-engined, massive piece of construction with a near 60-foot wingspan to carry only 250lb of bombs, at a good deal less than 80mph if it was fully loaded. To

Ernst Udet's third victory was one of the slowest machines in the sky in late 1916 but well over 1,000 Caudron G4 were built and successfully used by all the Entente air forces for long-range reconnaissance and bombing. The RNAS had it until it was replaced late in 1917 by the Handley-Page 0/100, although the French had withdrawn it from daylight raids a year before that.

modern eyes it looks decidedly odd, termed pod and boom design, a rounded gondola to carry pilot and observer, with tail attached by an open network of Meccano.

Udet should have put himself above and behind his large, relatively slow victim, dived down and ambushed his enemies before they knew it. Instead, he flew straight at them, head on, and came close enough to see the faces of the men he was supposed to kill. He who hesitates is lost, and young Ernst was definitely hesitating. The French observer felt no such qualms; he was rattling away with his single machine gun. Some of the bullets hit the Eindecker's wings and fuselage and a couple hit Udet, one knocking his goggles off, another shattering the windshield and cutting his face. Suddenly snapped from his trance, his only thought was to get the hell out of there. Superficially wounded but deeply ashamed, he vowed always to seek out danger and confront it.

Even so, his career as aerial assassin was slow to get moving. His first came on 18 March 1916 when he did what he should have done before and dived on his victim, in this case picked out from a large formation of French aircraft, a Farman 40, a primitive and obsolete machine, basically a Shorthorn smoothed out a bit. It went down as a flaming wreck but Udet's old squeamishness briefly resurfaced when he saw the observer fall from it and tumble to earth alone.

Ernst's next was a long time coming too, on 12 October 1916. Described as a Bréguet-Michelin bomber, this was probably the Mark 4, like the more successful M5 a pusher, and like the Caudron a two-seater pod-and-boom with Meccano out the back. At 80mph it was no match for the 100mph Fokker D3 he was now flying, imperfect though that machine was. In his reformed unit, Jasta 15, Udet scored again on Christmas Eve, a Caudron G4.

Udet had three more victories with Jasta 15 but didn't really hit his stride until joining Jasta 37, on a part of the Front with more activity. He had a new aircraft too, the Albatros D3, with which he knocked down fourteen more confirmed and one probable between August 1917 and March 1918.

Not that he always came out on top. He hadn't been long with Jasta 37 when he came across a flight of three Sopwith Camels. With little experience of this new enemy but knowing the Camel represented the next step forward in fighter design, the better part of valour would have been a discretionary run for it, but he stayed to do battle.

Under close fire from three Sopwiths, Udet tried to roll, sideslip and dive his way out of trouble, coming down from 13,500 feet to 9,000, where he levelled out to review the situation.

Neither gun worked. Both petrol tanks and the radiator were holed. With fuel spilling all over him and the engine still going, a fiery death seemed imminent.

With the engine off, the Englishmen could easily finish him, except, they hadn't followed him down. They would claim him as a victory. There was a German aerodrome not so far away but gliding to it would leave no room for making choices when he got there.

Forced to come in with a following wind, he missed the huts, somersaulted as he hit the ground, finished the wrecking job the RFC had begun and, shaken but not injured, thanked the gods of airmen and the manufacturers of the Albatros.

Before that, in May or June 1917, Udet had had his fabled duel with Guynemer. Details of this encounter seem to come only from Udet; Guynemer's biographer Henry Bordeaux, for example, writing with access to Guynemer's diaries, does not mention it.

According to Udet, the pair had an epic *Kurvenkampf*, each getting in the occasional burst of fire, with Udet noting a word painted on his opponent's machine, 'Vieux'. It was known that Guynemer called his mounts 'Vieux Charles' and had that painted on the side, just as Udet had 'Lo' painted on his, being his girlfriend's nickname. We may assume, therefore, that if Guynemer's eyesight was as good as Udet's, and that he had heard of a man with only five victories spread over a year, then each knew whom he was fighting.

At one point, according to Udet, his guns jammed and he tried to get them going again by standing up in his seat and thumping them. Guynemer flew by, noted the predicament of his potential fortieth or so Boche, suddenly came over all chivalrous, raised a hand in farewell and flew away. Of course, it may all be true, but Biggles wouldn't have done that and neither would Udet.

Udet heard news of the death of his old CO, *Staffelführer* Leutnant Heinrich Gontermann of Jasta 15, the famous balloon expert (eighteen of them out of his thirty-nine victories). He had been test flying Germany's answer to the Sopwith Camel, the Fokker DR1 Triplane, on 29 October, when the upper wing broke up. Although the machine was already on active service with a string of victories, another similar incident two days later grounded the Triplane until this problem could be solved.

In fact it never was entirely solved. The DR1 was not produced in large numbers and by mid-1918 its superb agility was largely made redundant by much faster Entente aircraft. Meanwhile, by the time Udet got his hands on one, the Dreidecker was the weapon of choice of Manfred von Richthofen. On a total of twenty victories confirmed, Ernst Udet was recruited by the master into *Jagdgeschwader 1*, hunting group/fighter wing number one, consisting of Jagdstafflen 4, 6, 10 and 11, also called the Flying Circus because it was formed to be mobile, ready to be sent where temporary/local air superiority was required by the army.

Udet was given command of Jasta 11 and led by example, flying more patrols than anyone else despite the fighter ace's curse, nerves shattered by battle, plus chronic earache. Even so, he had his twenty-first, a two-seater RE8, and his twenty-second was a Sopwith Camel, flown by a rookie Australian of 47 Squadron, Second Lieutenant Charles Maasdorp whose body was never found, despite Udet's claim to have landed beside the wreck and seen a single bullet hole in the head.

After his twenty-third, another Camel, on 6 April, he was ordered home for a rest by von Richthofen. A fortnight later the boss was dead and Udet returned as commanding officer of Jasta 4, to embark on a run of fourteen victories in just over a month, all of them French machines, SPAD and Nieuport fighters, Bréguet two-seaters, punctuated by an experience no British pilot could have had: a parachute jump. None of the Entente powers issued parachutes to aircrew in this war, except to balloonists. The French and the Americans allowed men to buy and carry their own chutes, but very few did so, while the Germans began providing them as standard equipment in the summer of 1918.

In late June, with his score up to thirty-five, Udet attacked yet another Bréguet and believed he had shot the observer. Closing in for the kill, apparently immune himself, he was surprised to see a man pop up behind the enemy gun and start firing to very good effect. Udet went into an involuntary dive, with all controls jammed or otherwise useless.

Looking down, Udet guessed he was at about 1,500 feet. Experience in these matters was very limited and not the subject of wide discussion in the mess; Udet was only the second or third German pilot to attempt a jump. He found that to stand up and leap out of a diving Fokker D7 was almost impossible but, with the ground rushing up towards him, not quite. He smashed against parts of his machine before falling free and, somehow, his chute opened with still another 500 feet to go.

There was another new experience in store: being in the middle of an artillery bombardment. As he landed, the ground was erupting and shaking all around him, the noise was deafening, and explosions knocked him over several times as he ran for safety, which he found with some infantrymen sheltering in a trench. After initial disbelief, a call on a field telephone brought transport back to the aerodrome. He was in the air the next day, knocking down a SPAD for his thirty-sixth, and the day after that he had more cause to note the progressive thinking of the German command in the matter of parachutes.

Udet's thirty-seventh was taken at around 19,000 feet, believed to be the highest of all conclusive fights, on 1

July 1918. He saw a Bréguet 14, believed to be using the latest equipment in photoreconnaissance, and went for it. Opening fire too far away gave the Frenchmen a chance to flee, but the D7 had maybe 20mph on them even at that height, and more bursts from closer quarters set the two-seater on fire. Udet, hardened as he was by so many fights, had to be moved by the sight of the two crewmen leaping from the flames, hand in hand, without parachutes, preferring that death to being burned alive.

Numbers forty-five and forty-six came on 8 August, two SE5A. Udet was in a small group on escort duty in his Fokker D7 later that same day when a Sopwith Camel came at him, guns blazing. Udet swiftly flipped, climbed and turned to get on the Camel's tail, pursuing it in a screaming dive. The RAF pilot pulled the same trick but managed to come up underneath Udet, so that when their mounts collided, he got the worst of it from Udet's undercarriage.

The Camel fell, not entirely out of control, and crash landed. Udet's machine held together long enough for him to get home and raise a glass to his forty-seventh.

The mutual respect that fighter pilots had for their enemies was mixed, at least in Udet's case, with a certain puzzlement about attitude. He thought the Englanders, anyway, lacked a certain seriousness, as if war was a sport, and reports odd conversations with felled opponents when landing beside them, when they'd say things such as 'Hello, old top. I'd have a smoke if I'd a cigarette to use this match on.'

Another vanquished pilot apparently said 'Jolly decent of you to let me off so easy. Topping sort of day. Have a cigarette. Craven A, good for the digestion and all that sort of thing. Funny damn war, isn't it? One minute you're up and the next minute you're down.'

Too cheerful by half, Udet thought. Germans were not built that way. The German attitude was calculating and ruthless, while the Englanders admired dash and style and were happy to go into battle with, as it were, their L-plates still affixed.

Udet had his final victories on 26 September 1918. Patrolling over Metz, he came across a formation of five DH9 returning from a bombing raid. One was straggling; Udet shot it down. When the others turned to attack, Udet flew straight at them and shot down another. The remainder fled and, for Ernst Udet, Blue Max, Knight's Cross, Iron Cross and various other awards, the war was over.

MANFRED, FREIHERR VON RICHTHOFEN, RIDING MASTER OF THE SKIES

The pop song about Snoopy and the Bloody Red Baron of Germany was quite wrong. Eighty men didn't die trying to end that spree; it was a great many more than that, as around two-thirds of his victories were over two-seaters, and some more of his victories were not counted officially.

A cavalry officer as the war began, von Richthofen became consumed by the flying disease. He wrote in his diary:

> The next morning at seven o'clock I was to fly for the first time as an observer. I was naturally very excited, for I had no idea what it would be like. Everyone whom I had asked about his

feelings told me a different tale. The night before, I went to bed earlier than usual in order to be thoroughly refreshed the next morning. We drove over to the flying ground, and I got into a flying machine for the first time. The draught from the propeller was a beastly nuisance. I found it quite impossible to make myself understood by the pilot. Everything was carried away by the wind. If I took up a piece of paper it disappeared. My safety helmet slid off. My muffler dropped off. My jacket was not sufficiently buttoned. In short, I felt very uncomfortable. Before I knew what was happening, the pilot went ahead at full speed and the machine started rolling. We went faster and faster. I clutched the sides of the car. Suddenly, the shaking was over, the machine was in the air and the earth dropped away from under me.

I had been told the name of the place to which we were to fly. I was to direct my pilot. At first we flew right ahead, then my pilot turned to the right, then to the left, but I had lost all sense of direction above our own aerodrome. I had not the slightest notion where I was. I began very cautiously to look over the side at the country. The men looked ridiculously small. The houses seemed to come out of a child's toy box. Everything seemed pretty. Cologne was in the background. The cathedral looked like a little toy. It was a glorious feeling to be so high above the earth, to be master of the air. I didn't care a bit where I was and I felt extremely sad when my pilot thought it was time to go down again. I should have liked best to start immediately on another flight.

Fearing that the war would be over before he could complete pilot training, he chose immediate posting as an observer over the trials of learning to fly. He was sent to the Russian Front, where he crewed with another sporting aristocrat like himself, the Graf Holck, who liked to take his pet dog with him on every flight. An uneventful but useful time there ended in a crash, and Manfred was sent to Ostend, to be observer/gunner/bombardier in the AEG G2, a twin-engined general purpose machine they called the 'apple barge'.

One fine day we started with our large battle-plane in order to delight the English with our bombs. We reached our object. The first bomb fell. It is very interesting to ascertain the effect of a bomb. At least one always likes to see it exploding. Unfortunately my large battle-plane, which was well qualified for carrying bombs, had a stupid peculiarity which prevented me from seeing the effect of a bomb-throw, for immediately after the throw the machine came between my eye and the object and covered it completely with its planes. This always made me wild because one does not like to be deprived of one's amusement.

We flew every day from five to six hours without ever seeing an Englishman. I became quite discouraged, but one fine morning (1 September 1915) we again went out to hunt. Suddenly I discovered a

Farman aeroplane which was reconnoitring without taking notice of us. My heart beat furiously when my pilot Zeumer flew towards it. I was curious to see what was going to happen. I had never witnessed a fight in the air and had about as vague an idea of it as it was possible to have.

Before I knew what was happening, the Englishman and I rushed by one another. I had fired four shots at most while the Englishman was suddenly in our rear firing into us like anything. I must say I never had any sense of danger because I had no idea how the final result of such a fight would come about. We turned and turned around one another until at last, to our great surprise the Englishman turned away from us and flew off. I was greatly disappointed and so was my pilot.

Both of us were in very bad spirits when we reached home. He reproached me for having shot badly and I reproached him for not having enabled me to shoot well. I had always believed that one shot would cause the enemy to fall, but soon I became convinced that a flying machine can stand a great deal of punishment. Finally I felt assured that I should never bring down a hostile aeroplane, however much shooting I did.

Our pleasant days at Ostend were soon past, for the Champagne battle began and we flew to the Front in order to take part in it in our large battle-plane. Soon we discovered that our packing-case was a capacious aeroplane but that it could never be turned into a good battle-plane.

I flew once with [Paul von] Osterroht who had a smaller machine than the apple barge. About three miles behind the Front we encountered a Farman two-seater. Osterroht flew with great skill side by side with the enemy so that I could easily fire at him. For the first time I saw an aerial opponent at quite close range... [he] had not noticed us at all for he did not fire back until I had my first gun jam. After I had fired my entire drum of 100 rounds, I could not believe my eyes, as all of a sudden the opponent went down in a peculiar spiral. He fell into a big shell crater; we saw it, standing on its nose, with the tail pointing to the sky. We had brought him down on enemy ground, otherwise I should have one more victory to my credit. I was very proud of my success. After all, the chief thing is to bring a fellow down. It does not matter at all whether one is credited for it or not.

The two-seater must have been relatively undamaged and worth recovering, because there is no French record of it being lost. In any case, if it had fallen behind German lines and been witnessed, it would have been scored to Paul von Osterroht, who had seven victories when he was shot down and killed by Sopwith Pup pilots of No. 3 Squadron RNAS.

Around this time, Manfred met Oswald on a train. He asked Boelcke how he did it, how he shot down so many enemy planes.

He laughed, although I was quite serious. Then he replied 'Yes, good heavens, it is quite simple.

I fly as close as I can, aim well, and then he falls down.' I just shook my head and thought to myself that I had done the same thing, but my opponent had not fallen down. The difference, to be sure, was that Boelcke flew a Fokker monoplane and I an AEG. I formed a resolution that I also would learn to fly a Fokker. Perhaps then my chances would improve.

In learning, he crashed his kite on landing from his first solo flight, and failed his pilot's test first time. Before passing it on Christmas Day 1915, he was briefly assigned as an observer to the new *Riesenflugzeug* project, the R-type Giant, with a five-man crew. In his memoirs he implies that he flew in this fantastical machine: 'From the beginning I took a great interest in the Riesenflugzeug. Strangely enough, flying in the gigantic thing made it clear to me that only the smallest aeroplane would serve my purpose as a combat pilot. Agility is needed and fighting is my business.'

This extraordinary behemoth, the Linke-Hofmann R1 Type, carried its four engines inside the fuselage, where they were attended by a flight engineer. Power was transferred to two propellers by chain drive. Two pilots and a wireless operator sat above the engines, while one or two bomb aimers/handlers were below with the petrol tanks. No guns were in the spec.

The firm of Linke-Hofmann had been known before the war for building trams and railway engines. The project was abandoned after both prototypes crashed, so if Manfred did fly in one, it wasn't on ops.

Anyway, in a history-changing moment, von Richthofen was transferred to a reconnaissance *Staffel* flying the recently acquired Albatros C type two-seater, and one day his destiny arrived at the 'drome, a Fokker Eindecker, and he just had to fly it. Another officer shared it with him. 'I flew it in the morning and he in the afternoon. Each of us was afraid the other would smash the crate to pieces.'

It was a justified fear. The other officer, Leutnant Hans Reimann, got in a fight with a Nieuport and lost. He survived but the aircraft did not.

'A few days later I was given another Fokker. This time I felt under a moral obligation to attend to its destruction myself.'

An engine failure forced Manfred down, and the machine was wrecked in a hayfield.

Meanwhile, there was the day job with the two-seater. Copying the French with their forward-firing machine gun on the top wings of their little Nieuport 11 Bébés, Richthofen had had a Spandau fitted to the top wing of his Albatros, so that he felt more like a fighter pilot and less like a chauffeur for the observer who managed the rear-firing gun. It was a clumsy-looking arrangement. Already the Albatros had an ugly assembly of engine and exhaust in front of the pilot's nose, but the Baron ignored the difficulties and his mess-mates' ridicule.

He took off on 26 April 1916 and flew towards Verdun, scene of slaughter and disaster for months. Over the lines he spotted a Bébé, a faster machine than his own normally but seemingly slower today. The Nieuport's gun was u/s so the Frenchman turned to flee. Richthofen chased and was catching up when, for the first time in anger, he pressed the button on the firing cable of his novelty gun.

'A short series of well-aimed shots and the Nieuport reared up and rolled over. At first my observer and I thought it was one of the many tricks the Frenchmen go in for.'

There was no trick but the machine fell in the French sector, with no German witnesses other than the airmen. Manfred could report it as shot down, and it would be noted as such, but it would not count on his scoresheet.

Meanwhile, Boelcke and Immelmann had become celebrities. Manfred wanted to be like them, and Immelmann's death did nothing to dampen his ambition, nor did writing off another Fokker in unforced error, but moving to the Russian Front as a bomber pilot postponed it. Still, he had a good time, relatively unopposed by few anti-aircraft guns and even fewer Russian fighter planes.

> At last we got into a quiet atmosphere. Now came the enjoyment of bombing. It is splendid to be able to fly in a straight line and to have a definite object and definite orders. After having thrown one's bombs one has the feeling that one has achieved something, while frequently, after searching the air for an enemy to give battle to, one comes home with a sense of failure at not having brought a hostile machine to the ground.

By August new units were being formed: Jagdstaffeln, hunting/pursuit squadrons. Boelcke was ordered to form Jasta 2; he recruited first his friend Erwin Böhme, and second a fellow he knew a little personally but more by reputation: Manfred von Richthofen. They set up near the Somme.

It was a time when the long-held German air superiority, due to the Eindecker, was coming to an end. Nothing had been able to stop the Fokker until the FE2B two-seater biplane arrived at the Front. It didn't look very modern, being a pusher with an open lattice framework behind the propeller rather than a closed-in fuselage, but it could do 90mph. It was often used as armed escort for reconnaissance aircraft as well as on missions in its own right, and the Germans were wary of it, even if its own crews, particularly the observers, had to perform a sort of circus act when attacking or defending.

Such aircraft were not generally fitted with safety harnesses, so when the observer stood up to fire his forward-pointing gun, he could grip that with his hands and brace his knees against the cockpit sides and hope that was enough to keep him on board while he swung his gun through its very wide field of fire.

There was a second gun on some machines, mounted on the centre section of the upper wing to protect against attack from the rear. While the German fired at the FE2 through his propeller, the FE2 pilot could be rather inhibited from taking evasive action by his observer standing in front of him, feet perilously balanced on the edges of his cockpit while he reached up to fire the rear-pointing gun.

The replacement for the Eindecker, the Fokker D3 biplane, was not good enough to make a difference, but the Albatros D type was. This had a more powerful engine to carry two Spandau guns and almost 1600 rounds, and yet keep up with the enemy. Von Richthofen's first confirmed victory was in one of these, over the comparatively large, cumbersome FE2B that he mistakenly called a 'Vickers two-seater'.

> He fired and so did I, but we both missed. Then the fight began. I tried to get behind him because I could only fire in the direction I was flying. This was not necessary for him, as his observer's flexible machine gun could fire in all directions. But this fellow was no beginner, for he knew very well that the moment I succeeded in getting behind him, it would be his last hour.

'This fellow' was nineteen years old, Second Lieutenant Lionel Morris of 11 Squadron. Mortally wounded and with his engine u/s, he still managed to land his aircraft. His observer, Captain Tom Rees, twenty-one, had been killed outright by von Richthofen's bullets.

Thus was counted number one in a series of eighty, which would make von Richthofen the highest-scoring ace of the war. It is certain that eighty wasn't the true number. It may well have been more, including those falling on their own side of the line; it could have been fewer, as witnesses were not required during the later stages of von Richthofen's career and fighter pilots will always tend to over-claim.

On the same day that Manfred chalked up number one, 17 September 1916, Böhme and Hans Reimann had their seconds and Boelcke his twenty-seventh. There was a good night spent in the officers' mess at Jasta 2.

So, Manfred von Richthofen had begun his odyssey that would make him the most famous fighter ace of all, truly ace of aces, conqueror of at least eight British pilots who were themselves aces and, uniquely for his kind, the inspiration for a terrible pop song.

A Martynside was followed by another FE2B, then a BE12 (single-seat version of the BE2C with a much more powerful engine), FE2B, BE12, so he was a fully accredited ace by 18 October, the day Boelcke was killed. He reached ten by November 20. Three days later, flying an Albatros D2, he came across and defeated a notable enemy in Lanoe Hawker (*q.v.*), the first British ace, who had won the DSO in April 1915 for his lone attack on the Zeppelin shed at Gontrode.

On sixteen, and feeling a little put out at not yet having the Pour le Mérite when Immelmann and Boelcke had theirs on eight, Manfred was posted as CO of Jasta 11- 'I would rather have had the Orden'- and, of course, the Blue Max telegram arrived. He set about organising his squadron to compete with his old unit, and reflected on his chances:

> In my opinion the aggressive spirit is everything and that spirit is very strong in us Germans. Hence we shall always retain the domination of the air. The French have a different character. They like to put traps and to attack their opponents unawares. That cannot easily be done in the air. Only a beginner can be caught and one cannot set traps because an aeroplane cannot hide itself. The invisible aeroplane has

not yet been discovered. Sometimes, however, the Gaelic blood asserts itself. The Frenchmen will then attack. But the French attacking spirit is like bottled lemonade. It lacks tenacity.

The Englishmen, on the other hand, one notices that they are of Germanic blood. Sportsmen easily take to flying, and Englishmen see in flying nothing but a sport. They take a perfect delight in looping the loop, flying on their back, and indulging in other stunts for the benefit of our soldiers in the trenches. All these tricks may impress people who attend a sports meeting, but the public at the battle-front is not as appreciative of these things. It demands higher qualifications than trick flying.

When the Bristol Fighter F2B arrived at the Front in April 1917, crew treated it as a normal two-seater, leaving the fighting to the observer, although it had a fixed, forward-firing gun. Once it was realised that it was better flown as a single-seater with extra armoury, this machine became one of the very best of the war. That realisation came too late for 48 Squadron, when their six brand-new F2B met five of von Richthofen's Albatros D3 on the 5th of Bloody April. Four of the Bristols went down in a half-hour dogfight, two of those claimed by Manfred himself as numbers thirty-five and thirty-six.

Therefore, the blood of English pilots will have to flow in streams.

Blood would have to flow in streams because the Red Baron understood the importance of military intelligence, and that his sole purpose was to kill in support of the army, the soldiers who could win victory.

Von Richthofen changed to a Fokker triplane (F1 version) in September 1917, then back to the Albatros, and again to the DR1 triplane, which could outclimb and out-manoeuvre all else but eventually was outdone for speed. Along the way he had each of his machines painted bright red, earning the nickname '*Le petit rouge*', and then he had all his *staffel* turned red. The days of the famous Flying Circus had arrived.

Towards the end, when the SE5A and the Sopwith Camel were creating air superiority for the Entente, Manfred knocked down two of the former and two of the sturdy but slow Armstrong-Whitworth FK8, but his speciality was the Sopwith.

In the evening of 20 April 1918, Manfred shot down two Sopwith Camels within three minutes, his seventy-ninth and eightieth victims as officially counted. That made nine Camels and a (Sopwith) Dolphin in his last fifteen victories.

Next day he led his fighter wing, his circus, to an area near Villers-Bretonneux, a small town in Picardy by the River Somme, which was about to witness the first tank-to-tank fight between British and German armour. This morning, however, the good folk of Picardy would watch something quite different, a dogfight between a dozen Sopwith Camels of the recently designated Royal Air

Force and a formation of rather more than twice as many Albatros D5 and Fokker Triplanes.

It turned into a terrific tangle, aircraft all over the sky, zooming in and out. A new Canadian pilot with 209 Squadron (previously No. 9 RNAS), Lieutenant Wilfred May, forgetting his orders to stay at 12,000 feet, dived on a German. By the end of the war, May would be an ace with ten victories plus three shared, but right now he found himself in the middle of the mayhem with his guns jammed. Spinning down and out of trouble, he levelled out over the River Somme and headed for home. Spotting what must have looked like a weakling, von Richthofen set off in pursuit, only to be chased himself by another Canadian, Captain Arthur Roy Brown, also of 209 Squadron RAF and another ace, at this point on six victories plus three shared.

Over the commune of Vaux-sur-Somme, Brown made his attack on Richthofen, not knowing who it was, and got in a good burst of fire that hit around the cockpit. His report states: '[I] dived on pure red triplane which was firing on Lieut May. I got a long burst into him and he went down vertical and was observed to crash by Lieut. Mellersh and Lieut. May. I fired on two more but did not get them.'

After the attack, Brown made a steep climbing turn to his left, while Australian ground forces fired at the triplane with machine guns. According to eye witnesses, the German seemed to resume his pursuit of May then slow down, half a minute or so after Brown's attack, to make a slow, flat turn and glide to the ground.

Brown was officially credited with his seventh solo victory, but later evidence suggests that Richthofen was hit by the ground fire, one bullet passing through his chest, a mortal wound but not immediately fatal. Australian soldiers, rushing to the scene, stated that Manfred was still alive, so we must assume that he actually landed his machine, which was only lightly damaged, before expiring moments afterwards.

A British pilot flew over the enemy aerodrome at Cappy and dropped a note informing the Germans of the Baron's death.

LIEUTENANT CLWYD WILLIAMS GOES HUNTIN', SHOOTIN' AND FISHIN'

Late in the war, Richard Clwyd Williams MC, a captain in armoured cars, took a demotion to lieutenant so that he could join the RFC as an observer. Around Christmas 1917 he was posted to No. 30 Squadron in Mesopotamia (modern day Iraq). No training was given. He wrote:

> We were the only ones out in Mespots at that time and suffered in having to do with obsolescent material. Two flights were camped at a riverside airfield at Ba'Qubah and the third at Ramadi on the Euphrates about a hundred miles away. Major de Havilland, brother of the famous Geoffrey, was with us at Ba'Qubah, and he had been flying since 1911.
>
> The Turks did not fly, so we had Huns against us, and we had the oddest collection of aeroplanes including Martinsyde single-seaters, two SPAD with Hispano engines, some BE2C and 2E, and the new RE8. The SPAD could do

over 80mph but the rest were slower, sometimes much slower. One time I went up to do a shoot (artillery spotting) with a distant gunner battery but there was a strong wind against us. After twenty minutes we had made less than a mile from our airfield.

When I first turned up, I was surprised at the warmth of my welcome until I realised that their observers had been lacking in machine gun know-how, and the pilots too were unversed in the intricacies of the Vickers and Lewis guns.

So, I was in demand as passenger and instructor, and they were very anxious to learn how to rectify any of the four usual stoppages when in the air. We also rigged up moving targets on the ground to practise on.

My first flight over the line was in a BE2C. This antique had a 90hp aircooled engine, and pilot and observer were armed with Lewis guns. One was fixed to fire forwards at an angle which would miss the propeller. Mine was rigged by my seat behind the engine, and it was quite a contortion to wriggle into position amid all the struts and wires, and when one did finally get set, the arc of fire was minimal unless one was prepared to shoot some of the aeroplane away.

We could send down by wireless but had to receive by visual signal. A wing would often intrude when trying to read Morse (by lamp or shutter) from the ground, or they would put out white strips of calico fashioned into codes which we were supposed to carry in our heads. If the artillery unit had no wireless receiver, I used to write the message on paper, put it in a small, weighted canvas bag with coloured ribbons attached, and sling it over.

My second trip was to drop a valise of clothing and essentials on the nearest Hun airfield at Kifri for one of our recently shot-down pilots. A parachute of sorts had been made and I had one hell of a struggle to get the thing out before it started to billow. We heard later, from the addressee, that it had landed right on the dot and the only casualty was a broken bottle of whisky.

We were to recco a Hun airfield at Kirkuk (in April 1918) and drop a few bombs if we could. Coming home, I spotted many Turks evacuating trenches, while about a mile away was a regiment of Indian cavalry, out of work but flying the usual HQ red pennant. They obviously didn't have wireless so I dropped a message bag, telling about the retreating Turks, also to keep our machine in sight because I would fire a Verey's light when we were over this most desirable target.

Then took place a most spectacular cavalry charge. Troopers and officers were going in with sword and lance, with us 200 feet above them, popping off with both our machine guns. I had only used about half a Lewis drum when I got a jam, so I grabbed my revolver and emptied that, then fired my Verey pistol at them. Bill (Lieutenant Frank Nuttall, known as Bill) meanwhile was wagging the tail of the RE8 and getting a good spray of bullets into the enemy when WHAM! We were hit through the main petrol tank. The engine stopped dead but Bill made a perfect landing well away from the Turkish gents.

We were smothered in petrol and why we didn't catch fire I'll never know. Bill had been shot through the foot so I nipped out and ran towards the rear elements of the cavalry shouting for a doctor-sahib. One rode up in a very short time and bound up the foot.

The RE8 had a small gravity petrol tank set between the centre section struts and below the top plane. The main pressure tank having been shot up, we could still run the engine for a while, on gravity feed, if the prop-swinging could be done by the untutored hand of the observer. With Bill back in the pilot's seat, I started the official patter: switch off, suck in. He played his part with an exaggerated switch-off movement so that I could pull down on the prop blades to feed the cylinders with gas.

I had hardly moved when the engine started with a roar. Fortunately I was not leaning into the arc so only got a smack on the hand instead of being decapitated. We took off, as I thought for our advanced airfield but to my surprise he turned back over the lines. Thinking he was a bit touched, I bellowed in his ear 'That way,' pointing for home. The reply was 'I've still got some ammunition in the belt so I'm going back to find the bugger that shot me.' He soon thought the better of it, turned back and in about thirty minutes made another perfect landing, by which time, with petrol flowing all over and into his wound, he was in no state to get himself out of the cockpit. The mechanics pulled him free and took him to the MO.

Unlike the squadrons on the Western Front, which had the whole of France behind them for supplies of supplementary delicacies, No. 30 Squadron on the banks of the Tigris had to be more imaginative if they were to improve their diet.

The river was plentifully stocked with the 'Tigris salmon' (the mangar, *Luciobarbus esocinus*), a large, bony fish, something like a cross between a barbel and a pike.

On our fishing shikahs, the simple drill was for the designated fisherman to sling a Mills bomb into the middle of the river from an upstream position. The explosion stunned the fish and they conveniently came to the surface, where the helpless creatures could be collected by volunteer swimmers from the squadron. Later we became lazy and employed Arab children. These artists would swim to the bank with three fish aboard, one held in the teeth by its dorsal fin and one in each hand.

Another source of supply at certain seasons of the year was the sand grouse. These came over in clouds and landed all massed together. They were easy for we cads to shoot from cars. Very good eating they were too.

One day, after a recco over the line, a pilot said he had seen thousands of geese on a patch of water a few miles out in the desert. We immediately organised a shoot. Two officers collected the squadron shotguns and I, being OC armoury, borrowed a Lewis gun, and we set off in a Crossley tender to drive slowly towards the target. Stopping a way short, the two sportsmen disembarked and made their way cautiously to the water. When I considered they had got into position on each flank, I opened up with the machine gun right into the mass of sitting geese, putting up the birds for the other two.

It was a particularly hot day and the mirage was making visibility poor but I did spot two figures coming towards me from a car. Naturally I thought they were my two and waved encouragingly. Then I saw that they had red tabs on their uniforms, and red hat bands. The General and his staff major were also out after the geese.

They had been taking cover from our bullets in a nullah, and didn't I know of the order forbidding shooting behind the lines? What was my regiment, etc etc?

I confessed to not having a regiment. I was in the Flying Corps and had certainly not seen any such order. The General reluctantly let me off with a warning although I had spoilt his shikah.

We three RTC blokes collected some geese corpses and were hailed as heroes back in the mess. And we sent a brace of birds to the General.

LADDIE AND BEN

India's only ace, Indra Lal Roy DFC, known as Laddie, was from Calcutta but was at school in England when the war began. He joined the RFC at eighteen in July 1917, and did well enough to earn his wings and be posted to 56 Squadron that October, where his flight commander became Captain Richard Maybery MC and Bar, who had fifteen victories credited at that point.

At first, Laddie did not look likely to emulate his leader and managed to write off his SE5A without severe injury to himself in early December. After being given time to recover, he was sent back to England for some refresher training, and so missed the end of his much loved commander, who destroyed his twenty-first opponent then ran into anti-aircraft fire and was brought down in flames.

In less urgent circumstances, on medical grounds Lieutenant Roy would probably not have been drafted back into active service, but six months later he was in France with 40 Squadron and reacquainting himself with the SE5A. Flying with him on patrol was Gilbert Strange, known as Ben, brother of the great Louis, under flight commander and famous Irishman Captain George McElroy DFC and Bar, MC and Two Bars, who was on thirty-five victories at the time.

Laddie's first was a Hannover C on 6 July, but his big day was the 8th when he had two Hannovers and a Fokker D7, one of the two-seaters shared with McElroy and Strange. On the 13th he shot down a Pfalz fighter and another Hannover, this also shared with McElroy and Strange, and on the 15th two D7. His mercurial career lasted six more days, with two victories taking him to ten, then a fatal fight with a D7 of Jasta 29. There's always somebody better or luckier and it seems that Laddie met up with Oberleutnant Harald Auffahrt, CO of Jasta 29, and became his fifteenth of an eventual thirty.

Lieutenant Roy was posthumously awarded the DFC:

'A very gallant and determined officer, who in thirteen days accounted for nine enemy machines. In these several engagements he has displayed remarkable skill and daring, on more than one occasion accounting for two machines in one patrol.'

George McElroy was felled by archie on 31 July, after scoring his forty-seventh victory that morning. Ben Strange lasted a bit longer but only racked up seven wins before he too met somebody better, becoming Martin Demisch's tenth and final victim. Revenge came the next day, when Demisch met 40 Squadron again and lost.

ACES OF ACES, AMERICAN STYLE

There was an unofficial title much celebrated in the newspapers of the USA: Ace of Aces. It was an expression used by other air forces too, but perhaps only the Americans made it formal enough to transfer it from man to man like an hereditary dukedom, and, as with hereditary titles, the holder usually had to die before the next man took his place.

There were 122 American airmen awarded ace status. Of course, most of them fought their battles late in the war. Of the thirty-one on five victories, quite a few never had the chance of more because the war ended, likewise the sixty-two scoring more than five but less than ten.

There are several candidates for the accolade of first

The first man to be given the title American Ace of Aces was born in France. Raoul Lufbery is seen here looking rather cool and, can we say, rather French, in his later Lafayette days.

American ace, depending on the criteria applied. The outright first in time was Gervais Raoul Lufbery, American citizen from Connecticut but born in France, American father, French mother, brought up in France until his late teens by his *grand'maman*. He had a two-year spell in the US Army, where he learned to speak English, and joined the Foreign Legion at the start of the war. He transferred to the French air service and scored his first on 30 July 1916. His fifth came on 12 October 1916 and all of his sixteen confirmed victories were with the French service. He had two unconfirmed after he transferred to command the United States Air Service 94th Aero Squadron.

Lufbery's would seem to be a better claim than Harold Hartney's, whose grave is at Arlington, born a Canadian but later a naturalised American. He reached his fifth and sixth victories with 20 Squadron RFC on 14 February 1917, so Lufbery was still one ahead at that point. It was an eventful day for Hartney as he was later shot down by the Red Baron. He survived that to become CO of USAS 27th Aero Squadron, with which he won one more. As he was pilot of a two-seater FE2D, all his RFC victories were shared with his observer, the man who fired the gun. Probably the best you could say is that he was the first member of the US Air Service born on the North American continent to become an ace.

Frank Baylies of New Bedford, Massachussetts was turned down by his own air force for poor eyesight so he joined the French. He scored all his twelve victories with the Storks escadrille, between 19 February 1918 and 31 May, reaching five on 12 April. He refused a commission with the USAS to stay with his French colleagues, and was killed on 17 June 1918 in a dogfight with Fokker Triplanes. This makes him the first ace to be born in the USA, although there is another contender.

David Putnam from Boston, Massachussetts, was flying with the French Escadrille 156 and by March 15 he had claimed five victories, almost a month before Baylies, but two of them were unconfirmed. Officially on three, he followed that with a string of eight unconfirmed victories, and was not fully credited as an ace until 2 June.

Baylies just beat William Thaw from Pittsburgh, Pennsylvania, whose first victory was way back on 24 May 1916, downing a Fokker Eindecker from his Nieuport, but whose fifth, a balloon, didn't come until 20 April 1918. However, he had two victories in 1917 that were unconfirmed, possibly because they occurred well into enemy territory. If you count them, he reached ace status with his third confirmed on 27 March 1918 and, in any case, he was the first to become an ace while flying in the USAS.

The usual route into the war for these volunteer Americans was via the Foreign Legion or in a noncombat role such as ambulance driver, from which they engineered a transfer to the French or British air services. Once trained, some of the 'Frenchmen' suggested an all-American squadron, commanded by a French officer, and after much deliberation the Escadrille Américaine, No. 124, came to be on 20 April 1916. Initially, under Capitaine Georges Thenault, there were seven American pilots, including William Thaw. Among later additions was Raoul Lufbery.

The unit became well known and the Germans protested at losing aircraft and crew to a neutral country, so the name was changed to Escadrille de Lafayette in December 1916.

The first all-American ace was Douglas Campbell, from San Francisco, of the 94th Aero Squadron. He and Lieutenant Alan Winslow shared the squadron's first official victory over an enemy aircraft on 14 April 1918, a Pfalz fighter, and Campbell went on to become the first US-born, US-trained, US Air Service pilot to score five, with a Rumpler on 31 May. He was badly wounded while scoring his sixth (shared) and missed the rest of the flying war.

So far, nobody reaching ace status had anywhere near enough victories to overtake Raoul Lufbery. Indeed, until 12 April 1918 he was the only confirmed American ace flying, and when he was killed, on 19 May, he was ace of aces but his constituency consisted of only two others, or three if you take Putnam's word, and we see no reason why not, or four if you remember the forgotten man William Lambert of Ironton, Ohio and 24 Squadron RFC, then on five.

On that day, a German two-seater flew low over the 94th's aerodrome, taking photographs. A junior fighter pilot took it on and was not doing very well, watched by Major Lufbery whose own plane was out of commission. Another Nieuport was standing on the field; Lufbery jumped in and took off in this unfamiliar mount. The scene was described later by Eddie Rickenbacker (see below).

> Luf fired several short bursts as he dived in to the attack. Then he swerved away and appeared to busy himself with his gun, which evidently had jammed. Another circle and he had cleared the jam. Again he rushed the enemy from their rear, when suddenly old Luf's machine was seen to burst into flames. A tracer bullet in the fuel tank. He passed the Albatros and proceeded for three or four seconds on a straight course. Then to the horrified watchers below there appeared the figure of their hero in a headlong leap from the cockpit of the burning aircraft.

Some say Lufbery jumped; some say he fell out. Without a parachute, the result was the same either way, but if he did jump he was ignoring his own advice. Rickenbacker:

> I remember a conversation we had with Major Lufbery on the subject of catching afire in the air. I asked Luf what he would do in a case of this kind, jump or stay with the machine? 'I should always stay with the machine,' Luf said. 'If you jump you certainly haven't got a chance. On the other hand there is always a good chance of slide-slipping your airplane down in such a way that you fan the flames

away from yourself and the wings. Perhaps you can even put the fire out before you reach the ground. It has been done. Me for staying with the old bus, every time!'

Lufbery was at 200 feet. No room for side-slipping but perhaps, he thought, the faintest chance of survival at 120mph?

The king was dead; who was the new king? He's usually given as Paul Baer, from Fort Wayne, Indiana, who joined No. 124 Lafayette and stayed with it as it was turned into the 103rd Aero Squadron, USAS, in February 1918. He scored his first on 11 March, his fifth on 23 April, and his ninth on 22 May when he was shot down too, wounded and taken prisoner.

With the benefit of hindsight, Wilfred Beaver of 20 Squadron RFC was a pretender to the throne with thirteen when Lufbery was killed, but he was British by birth, was a two-seater pilot so all his triumphs were shared with his observers, and he hadn't yet become an American citizen.

Succeeding Baer was Frank Baylies, who had nine confirmed at the time and went on to make twelve by the end of May. According to the American press, on June 17, Lieutenant Baylies and *Maréchals des logis* (Quartermaster-sergeants) Dubonnet and Macari were on their way home from a patrol when they saw four fighters that they took to be British and so carried on. This does seem odd, as the fighters were probably triplanes of Jasta 19 and the RAF, as it now was, had withdrawn the Sopwith Tripehound from duty.

Anyway, the ignored Germans set about Baylies and

sent him down in flames almost straight away. André Dubonnet had shared a victory with Baylies on 3 May and went on to become an ace himself.

Next in line of succession was David Putnam, who was on nine confirmed victories, as was Lambert but he wasn't in an American outfit and Putnam very likely had many more, with fifteen unconfirmed because they were so far behind enemy lines. He claimed two such on 12 April, three on 23 April, and four on June 5, which may have made five on the day with the one that was properly witnessed. Some of these missing victories must surely have been creditable, and Putnam's final score of thirteen can have done him no justice, in contrast to those victories which counted for other pilots when it was the observer who did the work, or who were given a full credit for a forcing down or an out of control.

Putnam's last victory, SPAD 13 versus Fokker D7, was late in the day of 12 September. About an hour later he met Georg von Hantelmann, also in a D7, only nineteen years of age but on his way to an undefeated total of twenty-five plus five unconfirmed, including French rugby captain Maurice Boyeau. Putnam became von Hantelmann's eighth.

On that day, Edgar Tobin, of San Antonio, Texas and the 103rd Aero, was on five plus one unconfirmed, and is usually crowned as ace of aces, although Francis 'Razors' Gillet, of Baltimore, Maryland and 79 Squadron RFC/RAF, was on six and would go on to twenty confirmed in his Sopwith Dolphin. William Lambert by now had eighteen wins in his SE5A but he was in hospital with battle fatigue and would be sent back home.

Tobin had a very short moment in the limelight but

at least did not have to die to step out of it, for he was overtaken on 15 September by the really unchallengeable American ace of aces, Eddie Rickenbacker, then on eight, only for another man to surge to the front three days later, Frank Luke, of Phoenix, Arizona, who scored five on 18 September taking him to thirteen.

Luke's whole flying career was brutish, short and, mostly, solitary. He came to the 27th Aero, The Eagles, under CO Harold Hartney, on 25 July 1918 but didn't begin his personal blitzkrieg until 12 September. He was an ace in three days, all balloons, and if he knew of the biblical stricture that six days shalt thou labour, he certainly fulfilled it, having thirteen victories by the end of his working week, including two balloons, two Fokker D7 and a Halberstadt two-seater all on the 18th.

Luke was not the usual officers' mess type, a working miner rather than a college boy – although brilliant at sport – and he had made few friends by telling everyone how he was going to win the war once he was allowed into combat. When he did get into the fight, he often ignored orders and conventions and much preferred to fly alone rather than follow squadron discipline.

He had a close pal, Joe Wehner, and they busted three balloons together, but otherwise his second priority, along with felling Germans, was to show his squadron colleagues that he was the best. Alas, his friend was killed on six victories on 18 September, reportedly flying guard as Luke attacked another balloon and failing to protect himself against Georg von Hantelmann.

Driven by this need to prove himself, Luke took down a Hannover two-seater and four more balloons in two days.

His dramatic end is described in a letter from the Mayor of Murvaux, Auguste Garre:

> The undersigned, living in Murvaux, Department of the Meuse, certify to have seen on the 29th of September, 1918, toward evening an American aviator followed by an escadrille of Germans in the direction of Liny, descend suddenly and vertically toward the earth, then straighten out close to the ground and fly in the direction of Briers Farm, where he found a German captive balloon which he burned. Then he flew toward Milly where he found another balloon, which he also burned in spite of incessant fire directed toward his machine. There he apparently was wounded by a shot from rapid fire cannon. From there he came back over Murvaux and still with his guns he killed six German soldiers and wounded as many more. Following this he landed and got out of his machine, undoubtedly to quench his thirst at the stream. He had gone 50 yards when seeing the Germans come toward him still had the strength to draw his revolver to defend himself. A moment after he fell dead following a serious wound he received in the chest.

The soldiers did not shoot Luke; he died from that single cannon shell in the chest. At this late stage in an apparently losing war, the Germans did not always maintain their precise behaviour towards fallen enemies, and they more or less threw Luke's body into a swiftly dug and shallow grave.

And it was eleven German soldiers he killed in strafing, not six.

Be that as it may, Eddie Rickenbacker was reassigned the title on 29 September, although it was not until 10 October that he surpassed Luke's eighteen, with two of his own on that day, both Fokker D7.

Rickenbacker was another untypical recruit to the USAS, not a college graduate but a clever mechanic and ex racing driver. He wriggled his way in and proved conclusively that you don't need a higher education to shoot down Germans. He also indicated that he and his fellow pilots were men, not supermen, when he said 'Courage is doing things you're afraid to do. There is no courage without fear.'

Even Rickenbacker himself must have acknowledged that he was lucky to get to the end, after a bad start and

Edward Vernon Rickenbacker poses in his SPAD 13.

illness preventing him flying during the summer of 1918, the busiest time of all.

When originally assigned to the 94th Aero, he had found a squadron with aircraft but no guns. By the end, he had twenty-six victories, three of them shared, making him the highest scoring American pilot of the war. His final two were balloons, at least one of which was on the ground in the late evening of 30 October. And then the war was over.

KAZAKOV OF THE RAF

Aleksandr Aleksandrovich Kazakov was from a Russian aristocratic family and, as befitted one so born, attended military schools and became a cavalry officer. Perhaps recognising that the future of the cavalry would be in the air, he had himself posted into the air service, learned to fly, and was a fledged pilot by the time the war began.

Things did not go well. The invasion of East Prussia, begun on 17 August 1914, dissolved into chaos and massive defeat in the Battle of Tannenberg. As with their French and British allies, the Russian Imperial Air Service had not really got around to the idea of armed aerial fighting, and Kazakov was desperate to find some way of knocking Germans and Austrians out of the sky.

He was stationed around what is now the border between Poland, Lithuania and Belorus, then disputed territory between the Austro-Hungarian Empire and Imperial Russia. As mentioned in an earlier chapter, Kazakov's first idea was to dangle grappling irons below his machine, hoping to rip holes in a presumably passive foe below. He might have known this wouldn't work, and in exasperation he resorted to another unsuccessful tactic he had heard about. In late August 1914, the world's first loop-the-looper, Pyotr Nikolayevich Nesterov, also in a Parasol and armed of course only with his service revolver, thought he could give an Austrian Albatros a whack from above with his undercarriage and perhaps rip a wing off. The two Austrians died in the resulting crash but Nesterov fell out and died of his injuries the next day.

Kazakov thought he could do it properly and, on 31 March 1915, he did, also on an Albatros two-seater. For whatever reason he didn't try it again, and the following year he transferred as commander to a unit equipped with the Nieuport 10, the obsolete two-seater bus converted to a single-seat fighter that Francesco Baracca disliked so much. Where the Italians failed, Aleksandr Aleksandrovich succeeded, shooting down two Albatros C types with his wing-top Lewis gun.

His squadron, the air detachment of the 19th Army Corps, was part of No. 1 Combat Air Group and Kazakov was made CO of that, after which he scored the two more victories he needed to be classed as ace. Posted to Romania, he carried on scoring, with two on 27 June 1917 and a wound to show for it. By late October of 1917 he was up to twenty, ten shared, but another twelve unconfirmed because they happened over enemy territory.

The Russian Revolution was under way and fast developing into a civil war between the Bolsheviks and the Tsarist White Russians. Kazakov knew which side he was on and joined the Slavo-British Allied Legion, a miscellaneous lot of misfits mixed with official forces, to fight with no known results against the new Soviet air force, then called the Workers' and Peasants' Red Air Fleet.

On 1 August 1918, Aleksandr Aleksandrovich was appointed Major Kazakov of the Royal Air Force (equivalent to Squadron Leader but the new ranks were not in use yet), and given command of a squadron at Archangel. That part of the war continued for another year but looked hopeless when the British and Americans began to lose interest. American forces left in April 1919. The Royal Navy was still in the Baltic but the RAF was being pulled out and there was a farewell dinner for the officers on 1 August.

Instead of going to that, a deeply depressed and unhappy Kazakov took off in a Camel, looped it, stalled it and crashed, watched by one James Ira Jones DSO, DFC and Bar, MC, MM, ace with thirty-seven victories who had volunteered to fight the Bolshies. In Jones's opinion, Aleksandr Aleksandrovich Kazakov 'brought about his own death and staged it in the most dramatic manner'.

LAST MEN DOWN

Flying was still a dangerous business even after the war, and twenty-five pilots who had won ace status during the fighting were killed in flying accidents in the year following the Armistice, 11 November 1918. Other post-war mortalities were mostly from injuries suffered in combat.

Remington Vernam, American ace (six victories) was shot down and badly wounded on 30 October 1918, and left behind by the retreating Germans. He died of his wounds on 1 December. German ace Friedrich Ritter von Röth (twenty-eight) shot himself on 31 December 1918, so depressed was he at Germany losing the war. Max Näther (twenty-six including ten balloons) was wounded on 27 September and died on 8 January 1919. Christian Mesch (thirteen) was killed in action sometime in 1919, fighting for the White Russians against the Bolsheviks.

Although fighting continued until the last minute of the eleventh hour, no aces died on that day, nor on the few days preceding. Captain Claud Harry Stokes DFC, flight commander with 57 Squadron, had five victories in the summer of 1918 in his DH4 two-seater bomber, four of them the redoubtable Fokker D7, the best German fighter of the war, plus one Pfalz D3, another top class single-seater. He was reported missing on 29 October 1918 and died from his wounds in German care in Belgium on 7 November 1918.

The last aces to be killed in action in the war were Australian Arthur John Palliser, known as Jack, from Launceston, Tasmania, age twenty-eight, and Thomas Charles Richmond Baker, from Smithfield, New South Wales, age twenty-one. They both died in the same action, on 4 November, in a pitched battle with the Jasta Boelcke.

Although much younger, Baker was the senior man, an ex-bank clerk who won the Military Medal plus Bar for acts of bravery while serving with the artillery at the age of nineteen. He joined the Australian Flying Corps in September 1917, got his wings in March 1918, was posted to 4 Squadron AFC and bagged two fighters, a balloon and a two-seater in his Sopwith Camel before Palliser got his first. Palliser may have come late to the flying war but soon made up for it, destroying a balloon and a D7 in his Camel before the squadron was re-equipped with the Sopwith Snipe.

This was a superior version of the Camel and the best Entente fighter of the lot, possibly the best fighter of the war after the Fokker D7, but only arriving at the Front two months before the end. It was not the fastest thing in the air but was very strong and agile and, with Jack Palliser in the cockpit, good enough to down five more of the D7, including three in one day, while Baker as captain and flight commander put down six in four days.

Compared to the early years of the war, the skies were now crowded with fighting aircraft, fleets of bombers, swarms of attackers on patrol. Battles unimaginable by Louis Strange and contemporaries were commonplace, as were combined operations far beyond anything possible in any number of Farman Longhorns. For instance, on 16 September 1918, two RAF squadrons and two AFC put together a formation of sixty-five aircraft to raid the German aerodrome at Haubourdin. With Clark and Palliser, No. 4 AFC went in first, to scatter and silence the opposition so that the bombers could work in peace, as it were. It is probable that this was the biggest air raid so far and it brought a new level of reward, some thirty or more enemy aircraft destroyed on the ground.

There was another mass effort on 4 October 1918. The Germans were retreating along the Lille–Brussels road (the modern N8) and the brief was to attack them on that section between Leuze and Ath, where there was also an enemy airfield. No. 4 Squadron provided fighter escort to the bombers and, on the way home, were intercepted by a flight of twelve Fokker D7 of the famous Jasta 2, the Jasta Boelcke.

Earlier in the year, the Germans had been losing pilots at a terrific rate in a period of Entente air supremacy. Replacements were rushed through. Experience was extremely important but very difficult to acquire, and so we may assume that twelve of the D7, probably flown by novices, would not worry 4 Squadron unduly even if they were outnumbered.

They would have known of Jasta 2's commander, *Rittmeister* (Cavalry Captain) Karl Bolle; up to the day before he had scored thirty-two victories. They could not have known that he was leading this formation and had already downed another two SE5A before lunch.

The Strutters turned to meet the Fokkers at around 13.10 and there was a mighty dogfight over the Tournai area. The Germans lost at least three: one shot down by Lieutenant George Jones DFC of Rushworth, Victoria, his seventh victory, two destroyed by flight commander Captain Elwyn King of Forbes, NSW, his twenty-fifth and twenty-sixth. King had ace status in the Snipe alone, these two making seven Snipe victories and him the highest Snipe scorer.

Bolle scored two; the Australians lost three. They were Lieutenant Parker Whitley Symons of Adelaide, South Australia, Lieutenant Palliser and Captain Baker. Baker definitely died that day, the other two are variously reported as dying on 4 and 5 November.

Bolle scored no more and a week later he and his Jasta surrendered their aircraft to the victorious Entente powers.

Envoi

Have you tumbled from the air until your wires were
    shrilly screaming, and watched the earth go spinning
    round about?
Have you felt the hard air beat your face until your eyes
    were streaming?
Have you turned the solar system inside out?
Have you seen earth rush to meet you and the fields
    spread out to greet you, and flung them back to have
    another try?
Would it fill you with elation to be boss of all creation?
    Well then do it, damn you, do it; learn to fly!

Have you fought a dummy battle, diving, twisting,
    pirouetting, at a lightning speed that takes away your
    breath?
Have you been so wildly thrilled that you have found

yourself forgetting that it's practice, not a battle to
the death?
Have you hurtled low through narrow, tree-girt spaces
like an arrow – seen things grow and disappear like
pricked balloons?
Would you feel the breathless joys of it and hear the
thrilling noise of it, the swish, the roar, the ever-
changing tunes?

from 'The Call of the Air' by Jeffery Day

FLIGHT COMMANDER MILES JEFFERY
GAME DAY, DSC

Jeffery Day was a flight commander with No. 13 Squadron,
RNAS, and was credited with five victories, all in a
Sopwith Camel, for which he was awarded the DSC. On
27 February 1918 he was shot down by a German seaplane
about twenty-five miles west of Dunkirk, landing in the
sea. Although he survived the encounter, by the time a
rescue could be mounted, no trace of him or his machine
could be found, and he therefore has no known grave.
Only three of his poems were published in his lifetime;
the extract above appeared in his posthumous collection
Poems and Rhymes, first published in 1919.

Index

Aircraft and air forces are indexed in two separate sections following the main index. *Page numbers in bold indicate illustrations.*

INDEX